Happy Birthday
Carolyn —
Love Nancy

D0395154

Henry Mitchell
on
Gardening

BOOKS BY HENRY MITCHELL

The Essential Earthman

Washington: Houses of the Capital

One Man's Garden

Any Day

Henry Mitchell on Gardening

Henry Mitchell
on
Gardening

HENRY
MITCHELL

WITH AN INTRODUCTION
BY ALLEN LACY

A Frances Tenenbaum Book

HOUGHTON MIFFLIN COMPANY

BOSTON · NEW YORK

1998

FOR SUSAN DAVIS

For information about permission to reproduce
selections from this book, write to
Permissions, Houghton Mifflin Company,
215 Park Avenue South, New York,
New York 10003.

Library of Congress Cataloging-in-Publication Data
Mitchell, Henry, 1923– .
Henry Mitchell on gardening / Henry Mitchell.
p.   cm.
"A Frances Tenenbaum Book."
ISBN 0-395-87821-7
1. Gardening. 2. Gardening — Washington
Region. I. Title.
SB455.3.M574   1998
635.9 — dc21   97-35353   CIP

Printed in the United States of America

The drawings by Susan Davis are used by permission.
Copyright © 1983–1993 by Susan Davis.

Book design by Robert Overholtzer

The material in this volume originally appeared, in
slightly different form, in the *Washington Post*

QUM 10 9 8 7 6 5 4 3 2 1

Contents

Introduction by Allen Lacy • ix

J A N U A R Y

When a Bloom Looms Large in Memory • 3
In Winter's Adversity, the Hardy Gardener Flourishes • 5
The Entanglements of Sweet Peas • 6
By the Persian Example • 9
Weather Soon Withers a Gardener's Innocence • 11
A Fig for All Seasons • 13

F E B R U A R Y

Roses Are Red, but Violets Are Bloomin' Lovely • 19
Sowing Seeds of Exotic Abandon • 21
Daffodil Delight • 24
Protect Us from Plants • 27
Bright Spots in the Shade • 30
Good Sense Has Little to Do with Gardening • 32
That Growing Sense of Frustration • 34
Winter Has Sprung • 36

MARCH

Weathering Winter's Chill • 43
Correcting the Mistakes of Mother Nature • 45
There Is Much to Be Done, We Must Get to It • 47
The Growing Anticipation of Spring • 50
Coming Attractions • 52
Support for the Red, Round, and Ripe • 54
Right at the Start • 58

APRIL

Spring Is the Time of a Thousand Tasks • 63
Dalliances with the Dahlia • 65
Facing Up to the Cold Facts • 68
Give Me Strength — It's Spring • 69
Thomas Jefferson, an Optimistic Gardener • 71
Gardening Pains and Pleasures • 75
Living to Grow Another Day • 76
Budding Romance • 78
Not Everyone Wants to Go Whole Hog into Gardening • 82

MAY

The Perfect Moment • 87
The Cicadas, Bringing Their Sweet Symphony • 89
Stopping to Smell the Rugosas • 92
The Gardener's Life Is Full of Woe • 94
The British Deal with Downpours • 96
After the Rain, a Deluge of Tasks • 98
Brave Spikes of Flowers • 101
The Best-Laid Plants • 103
Where Iris Is, I'm Smiling • 105
Rosy Outlook • 108

JUNE

The Ivy League • 113
Fare of the Dog • 115
How Does Your Garden Grow? Any Way You Choose • 118
The Computer as Gardener's Friend • 121
The Hard Way, Firmly Planted • 122
Contemplating Small Illusions • 124
Heeding the Garden's Call of the Wild • 127
Working the Bugs Out • 129
A Little Work, a Lot of Glory • 130

JULY

Gardening Is a Long Road • 135
Sunflowers and Memories • 138
Stalks and Bonds • 140
Plants That Make Their Own Elbow Room • 142
Every Garden Needs a Weed Patch • 144
Surrendering to the Ceiling Fan • 145
Keeping Watch on the Water Lilies • 148

AUGUST

A Gardener's Weather Wonderland • 155
The Wings of August • 157
Things Are Doing Better Than Expected • 160
The Topic Is Tropicals • 162
Pleasures of Plants by the Pool • 164
Awaiting the Last Blaze of Summer • 166

SEPTEMBER

Bulb Essentials • 171
The Beauty of Vines and Weeds • 173
Trailing Away from Summer • 176

Of Mice and Specimens • 178
Houseplants and Other Migrants • 181
A Life's Garden, in Full Sum • 183
Friends at Season's End • 186
Arches of Triumph • 188
One with Staying Power • 190

OCTOBER

Autumn Tasks and Master Plans • 195
Loving Blooms: Better Late Than Never • 198
The Bloom from Buried Bulbs • 200
A Garden of Choice • 202
The Fifty-Year Itch • 205
Weathering the Winter • 207

NOVEMBER

Support Groups on High • 213
The Outer Limits of Inner Space • 215
The Cold, Hard Facts of Autumn Planting • 216
The Vices and Virtues of Climbers • 217
Be It Blotch or Brilliance . . . • 219
When Perfect Isn't Good Enough • 221
Among the Berry Best of Bushes • 223

DECEMBER

The Budding Holly Story • 229
The Latest Dirt on the Garden's Doings • 232
The Beauty of Natural Selection • 233
The Imperfect Gardener • 235
Potted Perspicacity • 239
In Gardening, Timing Is the Key • 241

Introduction by Allen Lacy

For a couple of decades the luckiest gardeners in the nation were those who subscribed to the *Washington Post*. Every Thursday they could turn to Henry Mitchell's "Earthman" column to find out what was on his mind that week and what was going on in his garden in the District of Columbia. At a time when most garden writing was lethally dull and as impersonal as a committee report, Henry Mitchell was the great exception. He was often funny. He was always passionate, for his loves were many, although by the evidence he was especially enamored of bearded irises, roses, and dragonflies. He was endlessly quotable, whether he was telling his faithful readers that "marigolds should be used as sparingly as ultimatums" or reminding them that "to go from winter to summer you have to pass March." Many of his readers clipped and saved his columns. I know, for friends in the Washington area often photocopied and sent them to me, knowing I would appreciate them. And I did. Henry Mitchell was the best garden writer in America, but he was more than that. He was a master essayist, with such a highly distinctive voice and style that his newspaper pieces didn't really need a byline. Two or three sentences were sufficient to make it clear that Mitchell had written them.

Those of us who were unable to read his "Earthman" columns when they first appeared have rejoiced that many of them have been collected in book form, first in *The Essential Earthman* (1981), then in *One Man's Garden* (1992), and now in *Henry Mitchell on Gardening*. These books will continue to find and delight new readers long into the coming century, for they are classics. I can make this claim without fear of being contradicted, for Henry Mitchell is no longer with us. Were he alive, he would almost certainly say, "Classics? No, the books were just old newspaper columns, nothing more."

The three books give no clue that their author did virtually nothing to bring them into print, but his wife, Ginny, loves to set the record straight. When John Gallman of the University of Indiana Press approached Mitchell about publishing the columns that became *The Essential Earthman,* he had to go to Washington himself to collect the columns, and he, not the author, decided which ones would go into the collection and in what order. Later, when Ginny Mitchell found four unanswered letters from publishers expressing interest in another "Earthman" collection, her husband said, "No one wants to read these things; they're worthless." Ginny disagreed and offered to buy the rights, and the deal was made; Henry sold her the rights for one dollar. All Americans who love to read and who love to garden are the richer for this remarkable transaction.

I can think of no other writer so innocent of self-importance. There is an explanation, however. Henry Mitchell loved the English language as much as he loved roses and dragonflies, and he loved the works of William Shakespeare in particular. Shakespeare was the standard he judged himself by, and according to that standard he believed that he was only a journalist. Shakespeare was universal. Henry Mitchell considered himself to be merely local and parochial.

He was wrong about himself, of course. The truly universal turns out to be precisely the local and the parochial — the beastly days of deep winter or high summer, the marauding insect enemies, the orange marigolds that offend the eye when they're planted right next to annual salvias of fire-engine red, the grace that comes on the air with the sweet and heady perfume of roses, the bright visitations of dragonflies. Henry Mitchell knew all these things and wrote of them. In his pages we can find them — and him, and us.

Henry Mitchell was born in Memphis, Tennessee, the son of a prominent physician. He attended the University of Virginia in Charlottesville, but his career as a student was interrupted by military service during World War II. After the war he married Helen Virginia Holliday. For two years the Mitchells lived in Washington, where he began his newspaper career as a copy boy for the *Washington Star*. Later they moved to Memphis, where he became a columnist for the *Commercial Appeal*, a position he held for some twenty years. In 1970 he and his wife and their daughter and son moved back to Washington, where he was a reporter for the *Washington Post*.

Mitchell's career as a garden writer began in 1973, when he began his weekly "Earthman" column. Three years later he undertook another column, "Any Day," which dealt with any topic that struck his fancy. When he retired in 1991, he gave up that column, but he continued to write and delight his "Earthman" readers right up to his death in 1993.

No occupation is so delightful to me as the culture of
the earth and no culture comparable to that of the garden.

— Thomas Jefferson, 1811

In 1937 an uncle took me to the New York Botanical Garden to see this astonishing creature.

January

When a Bloom Looms Large in Memory

SOMETIMES A SINGLE FLOWER is enough — enough to be remembered clearly for more than half a century — and while the flower I speak of, *Amorphophallus titanum,* is not for us regular steady gardeners, the point is still the same, that even in a city garden a single daffodil or water lily or iris or rose may be so beautiful that it is remembered always.

Once I had a bloom of unearthly beauty on a daffodil, 'Wedding Bell', and while that variety is hardly in the running for "most beautiful daffodil," that one flower was glorious beyond reason. Other flowers of that variety were nice enough but nothing to go mad over.

There are individual roses and irises, individual blooms, that so far surpassed the usual and expected performance for that variety that I have never forgotten them. And the message here is that no matter how small the garden, it is large enough to produce a flower that the gardener will value in his memory long after he has forgotten whole fields of *auratum* lilies.

An allusion I once made to the great krubi, as the amorphophallus is called in its native Sumatra, inspired a number of gardeners to ask for more details about it. More than one person doubted that such a flower existed. Such is distrust in America today.

When I was a lad in 1937 an uncle took me to the New York Botanical Garden in June to see this astonishing creature. The garden had acquired a corm from Sumatra in 1932, and although it weighed sixty pounds it did not flower for five years.

I once spent a few hours with the late Thomas H. Everett, senior horticulture specialist at the garden. He was a remarkable man who single-handedly wrote the multivolume *New York Botanical Garden Encyclopedia of Horticulture.* During the happy day we spent wandering about the garden, I mentioned the 1937 flower, and to my surprise it turned out Everett himself was responsible for its care. Later he mentioned the Sumatran beauty in his encyclopedia, which is by long odds the best thing of its kind I have found.

He said the plant had flowered in the West probably only on six occasions, first at Kew in London in 1926 and second at New York in 1937, and that New York flowering was stunning beyond the others.

During the five years the corm grew in its wooden tub (a three-foot cube by 1937, as smaller tubs did not do) it produced from time to time a single leaf, which in time died down, to be followed a few weeks later by another single leaf. The largest leaf was more than six feet tall with a spread of ten feet.

The tub was set just a few inches above a sunny pool in a "stove" house designed to accommodate the giant South American water lily *Victoria amazonica,* but even that amazing plant seemed ordinary when the amorphophallus flowered.

The corm, now weighing an estimated one hundred pounds, began to sprout in early April 1937, and by May the shoot was forty-two inches tall. Clearly it was not going to be another leaf but at long last the anticipated bloom.

By the week of June 8 the spadix, the spike in the center of the flower, was eight feet five inches high. The inverted-bell-shaped part of the flower was forty-nine and a half inches in diameter, the exterior green and the ribbed interior purple-black. It was about June 10 when I saw the flower, and while there was a slight stink, it was nothing like the run-for-your-life stench of the Kew flower eleven years earlier.

The true flowers are massed along the tall spadix, as in other members of the arum group such as Jack-in-the-pulpit, Italian arum, and calla lily, but these are not noticeable.

The flowers of the amorphophallus were hand-pollinated, but not a single seed resulted. Pieces of the corm, which by now weighed 113 pounds, were cut off in an effort to propagate the plant, but without success; the plant died after flowering. I felt lucky to have seen it, as the plant is for all practical purposes never seen even in large botanical gardens, thanks to the difficulty of raising a corm to one hundred pounds and the need to keep it hot and moist with periodic drafts of manure tea.

This may be more about the flower than some gardeners wish to know, but I will say I was somewhat hurt that readers would think I made the thing up. The truth is that plants are so varied and so astonishing, and ordinary knowledge of them is so slight, that a camellia or a lily or a twenty-year-old willow two inches high will strain the belief of many.

In Winter's Adversity, the Hardy Gardener Flourishes

THERE IS A DANGEROUS DOCTRINE — dangerous because it precludes endless gardening pleasures — that every plant in the garden should be disease-free, bug-free, hardy to cold, resistant to heat and drought, cheap to buy, and available at any garden center.

The result of this notion is that there are actually gardens in this extremely favorable and extremely easy gardening climate in which all you see is a patch of damned roadside weeds such as that 'Goldsturm' rudbeckia.

I dislike that flower not so much because it is weedy (for after all I love such weedy creatures as bouncing Bet, daturas, sunflowers, and so forth) but because the rudbeckia proclaims that the gardener is going to settle for foolproof things. And sure enough, the rudbeckia will never break your heart like the twelve-foot camellias that die in February or the much-babied rose 'Maréchal Niel' that is killed outright on one disastrous Christmas Eve.

No need to mulch that rudbeckia or give it a bit of burlap, as you might do for either of the hardy palms of Washington. And certainly no need to bring it indoors like the puya, furcraea, or clerodendrum, or to give it a brick wall for shelter, as you do for Brazilian dawn flowers or white solanums or the night jasmine.

After some decades, when a gardener looks back, it's better to have rejoiced in sweet peas (which are extremely chancy beasts here) and delphiniums and tuberoses and oleanders and jasmines and much more, than to have settled for the hardiest toughest dullest plants of the Western world. It really is better to have loved and lost than never to have loved at all.

The Entanglements of Sweet Peas

❧ GARDENERS IN MID-JANUARY commonly like labor-intensive projects (such as raising sweet peas) that come to nothing but that keep them happily occupied. Otherwise they do damage to many plants with fitful pruning or by covering them with plastic sheeting (beneath which the plant sweats, steams, and dies).

So I shall give a time-tested set of directions for sweet peas. I have tried them myself and can say plainly that the results are hardly worth the effort, unless the gardener likes to astound people with a handful of sweet peas in May.

To begin with, sweet peas are not traditional flowers for Washington and the South generally, which is one reason the gardener is determined to have them. Ages ago a friend occasionally sent us laundry boxes of sweet peas raised in a field in northern Mississippi. They all burned up in June, I think, but for some few days they were glorious.

The strain popular today is called 'Galaxy', and it bears summer heat well, though it is an optimistic gardener indeed who hopes to have flowers after mid-July in Washington. This strain has the usual range of sweet pea colors — lilac, rose, pink, near-scarlet, purple, and white. The flowers are supposed to be fragrant, but it takes some imagination to detect it.

There are still available old varieties of sweet peas, usually sold in a mixture, that are supposed to be strongly fragrant, though the flowers are duller in color and less elegant in shape. I smelled some of these in London and found little fragrance, but they are worth trying if scent is what you want.

A strain called 'Snoopea' has been a sensation in England. These are dwarf plants that do not need to be supported and the vines do not have those troublesome tendrils. Regular sweet peas lean this way and that, their tendrils catching on to nearby sweet pea plants so that a fine tangle results.

I think it would be worth trying sweet peas beneath climbing roses, though success is not promised.

Once I grew sweet peas in a whiskey barrel and led the vines into a big yew. They sulked. But I confess they had a hard time with competition from *Nicotiana sylvestris*. That is a wild tobacco plant, growing to six feet, and I had not quite allowed for its enormous leaves, and the sweet peas did not flourish. They did well enough in the barrel another year without the tobacco plants but stayed on some stakes I had set in the barrel and had nothing to do with the yew. My original scheme, which dreamed of sweet peas in beautiful colors popping out here and there amid the dark green yew branches, came to naught.

Sweet peas like well-manured earth. It's a good idea right this minute to spread horse manure four inches deep on a well-dug bed, digging in the manure when weather permits.

All this presupposes you have space somewhere for a bed with nothing in it. In my case, the beds are stuffed with spring-flowering bulbs, and little spaces are left for tomato plants to go in at the end of April. I wonder if sweet peas could be planted while the daffodils and tulips still have fresh leaves, and if the vines would grow up the wire tomato cages without doing too much damage to the tomatoes.

But back to the directions. If seed is to be planted outdoors, the right time in Zone 7 is the second half of February or, failing that, early in March. One seed every six inches is plenty, and even then every other plant may well be pulled out for an ultimate spacing of a foot between plants.

The plants will not grow much before April, but then the advantage of early sowing will be apparent. It can happen that the seeds sprout soon after sowing and that warm days follow, then severe freezing. It helps to strew evergreen branches among the young sweet peas for a tempering effect.

I have planted the seeds outdoors in November but lost the batch in late January, and it is possible to fail from February-planted seeds also. Nothing is guaranteed.

If seed is planted as thinly as recommended here, you will have enough to make a planting around Valentine's Day; then, if disaster strikes, you can plant again in March. In any case the little vines will promptly start to climb and should be given twiggy sticks to get started. Ultimately the sweet peas will go to six feet or even more in rich deep beds.

Fanatics used to dig sweet pea beds three or four feet deep and work in rotted manure and various odd elements. But since 1900, two feet deep has been considered enough digging, and I think fourteen inches is better than nothing. I know some gardeners will simply not try at all if they think two feet is required.

Another way to grow sweet peas is in barrels or tubs or pots (ten inches wide at a minimum, and bigger is better) planting twelve seeds to the pot.

I have tried them both in large pots (fourteen inches) and half barrels. Even in large pots the vines will need watering every day from late spring onward. Also, however grown, the flowers must be cut off before they go to seed. Flowering stops once seed is set, as I proved to my satisfaction one year.

Seed can be started indoors if planting outdoors in February strikes you as foolhardy. Early March is soon enough, and four-inch pots with a single seed in each work well. Once I planted two seeds in each pot and then had to pull out one of the resulting plants. Pots should be kept two to four inches below fluorescent lights. If planted in January or February the plants will be far too tall and spindly to plant out in April.

If seeds are planted in larger, say six-inch, pots, the little vines will promptly tangle and be one clotted mess by April. Also, plants suffer if they have to be divided, so try growing them individually.

Too much is made of summer heat, perhaps, as one year I had flowers till Labor Day, and the varieties were not heat-resistant but leading exhibition varieties from England. I have not tried sweet peas on a chain-link fence, not having one, but they would be perfect there.

By the Persian Example

THE PRINCIPLES of the Persian garden are ideally suited for town gardens in regions utterly different in climate from the desert land in which they originated. Not many gardeners want a garden that shouts "Persia" at them, but a garden may be essentially Persian in design without Oriental touches in the way of Islamic tiles, water basins shaped like lotuses, and so on. The details can be quite Western.

The essential nature of Persian gardens is enclosure — the world shut out — with a dominant emphasis on water and enough foliage to suggest an oasis. The cost of high walls is prohibitive, but such ordinary (and marvelous) plants as native red cedar and holly will easily make walls of green sufficient to serve the purpose. The practical point of Persian water tanks and channels is irrigation, and that is not necessary in most American gardens. Still, our gardens are hot as the hinges for that part of the year when they should be used the most, and nothing is better than a fish pool and a shaded bower to view it from.

A kind of summerhouse, which can be as simple as wooden posts and a roof of wooden trellis, could be built by the house entrance to the garden. It could be paved with brick set right on the dirt, and in a small garden, perhaps only twenty-five by forty feet, the paving could continue, instead of grass, to a raised pool for water lilies and fish.

The pool does not need elaborate pipes and drains. It does not need anything at all, and can be drained and cleaned once a year or once every two years. It can be as small as necessary, but ten by twelve feet is not too large for the space being considered here.

On the summerhouse or arbor nothing is better than a grapevine. Nothing makes better shade, but such vines as actinidia, akebia, clematis, wisteria, trumpet vine, and honeysuckle are all obvious choices. If you preferred, you could have a rosy honeysuckle at one side and keep the other side free for annual vines. The moonflower (*Ipomoea alba*) would be agreeable if you sat in the garden much on summer nights, or morning glories might do for those gardeners who arise at five A.M. Cardinal climber, nasturtium, eccremocarpus, cucumber, gourd, or virtually any other climber that dies in the winter could be planted on one side of the sitting pavilion to go with the clematis or honeysuckle on the other side.

Flowers in such a garden should be of great beauty, as there cannot be many of them in a twenty-five by forty-foot garden. Roses, lilies, daffodils, irises, tulips, and crinums all come to mind, in narrow borders beneath the green walls, and at the edge, right against the pavement, any number of modest little things could be worked in — *Brodiaea uniflora*, arabis, alyssum, sedum, epimedium, or dwarf annuals such as nasturtium.

By keeping the trees (not really trees at all, but eight-foot junipers and hollies or yews used as a hedge) at the boundaries of the garden, and by keeping the center paved solid with brick or a substitute, with the big pool for water lilies and fish, the garden would not seem absurdly crowded. If you thought the brick paving looked overly generous, you could set a few tubs about with, say, *speciosum* lilies or angel's-trumpets or figs or bananas in them.

Plenty of luxuriant growth, a glittering patch of water with red fish swimming about, and a place to sit and admire it all — these are the essence of such a garden.

The Persians never counted on flowers in the summer. Their flowers came after the snows melted and lasted through the roses — altogether about a hundred days. Through the hot summer they counted only on cool shade and water and maybe some colorful tiles. We, of course, have wonderful water lilies that they did not, and Japanese anemones for the fall, and maybe some autumn crocuses and sternbergias. Chrysanthemums, too, if you wanted to give space to them.

There is nothing wrong with concrete, by the way. It need not look like a sidewalk. Earth colors (yellow oxide of iron makes a soft buff color) can be added to the dry mix, or the mix can include sphagnum peat so that it weathers to look like sandstone. So don't feel bad if cut stone or even brick seems to be too costly.

Most people would never know the garden was Persian in origin. A thing the Persians did that I very much like was to plant fruit trees among the cypresses. Peaches, pears, and plums all look fine with our red cedars and hollies, and the evergreens give weight to the otherwise too soft and too ordinary look of the fruit tree foliage.

Weather Soon Withers a Gardener's Innocence

THE SOONER THE GARDENER loses certain kinds of innocence the better, and there is no better place to begin with than the weather.

There is a type of spring, terrible and wonderful at once, in which January and even February are disarmingly mild, only to be followed by weeks of incredibly cold days in which the earth itself seems to shrivel and go dormant.

Those who love the daffodil and follow its odd fortunes know all this quite well. In the days before civilization collapsed and the Royal

Horticultural Society gave up its daffodil yearbooks, we could read (ten years out of eleven) how terrible the season was.

In 1969, for example, "Although this has been the latest flowering season we have had for many years, at one time it looked as if it would be one of the earliest." As a result, "it was obvious that we should not have any outdoor flowers" for the daffodil show in early April. "I have never seen such frost damage, it really was quite frightening," and every contributor rattles along with the same tone of injured righteousness. Beneath all the complaints is the sense that the weather has been not only bad but unfair. And wicked.

So you wonder how, in such a season, there can be photographs of daffodils that seem to have grown in Paradise.

No sooner does a contributor to the yearbook complete his accusations and lamentations than we find the surprising comment, "The very odd daffodil season therefore lasted twenty-four weeks." A few pages further on, "almost certainly the finest display of exhibition daffodils ever seen."

So which was it, the worst season, with unbelievable frost damage and unspeakable weather, or a season presenting the finest display of top-quality daffodils ever seen in this world?

Both, of course. The season that was going to be the earliest in years was the latest in years. There were no flowers to be seen in early April, the date of the great show. So of course at a later improvised show there was "the finest display ever seen."

In a perfect season many flowers are mediocre, and in a terrible season many flowers are of unearthly beauty. In the spring garden, things even out. The most perfect springs are heavy with bitter disappointments; the worst springs are bright with startling perfections.

The kind of innocence that is best lost quickly is the simple-minded belief that spring will be lovely. It will not. It will be dreadful. The equally stupid innocent belief that in a cold dismal spring everything will be wretched must also be outgrown, as again and again we are obliged to acknowledge "the finest display ever seen."

These paradoxes are by no means the hallucinations of unbalanced gardeners but the straight and true reports of steady judges with unmatched experience.

When the gardener loses (as his experience sooner or later forces him to lose) his innocence and sweet dreams about the spring and the daffodil season, he then is able to detect in the real world of outrageous weather and dashed hopes the finest display ever seen.

One of our poets spoke of Lucifer falling back when faced with the army of unalterable law. But of course we gardeners are well beyond any prince of Hell, as we flourish in the face of alterable, unpredictable, outrageous law.

Whatever this coming spring brings, early or late, freezing or blazing, the properly seasoned (greatly abused) gardener is well aware that in some ways (not immediately apparent to the innocent) it will be the most beautiful and tender season ever beheld in the history of the world.

A Fig for All Seasons

EVERY GARDEN should have its own grapevine and fig tree. Often the inexperienced gardener is afire to plant an apple, cherry, plum, or pear, supposing in his innocence that he'll get something fine to eat. It is far otherwise. The two fruits that are likely to produce something fit for the table are the fig and the blueberry. Sometimes the grape and the raspberry, blackberry, or boysenberry give good results, though dessert-quality grapes will require as many as ten applications of spray throughout the season.

Back to the fig. I have never encountered disease or bug problems on the fig, and surely it is the prince of fruit trees from Washington or Philadelphia southward. There will come winters, however, of such severity that the tree (more often a shrub the size of a crape myrtle) will be killed back, even killed to the ground. When this happens there will be a year or two without fruit, but the plant will eventually recover, provided a relatively hardy variety has been planted.

There are dozens of varieties of fig, but not all of them are hardy outside California and similar warm, dry places. In Washington the usual variety for the garden is 'Brown Turkey', which is often said to be the hardiest fig, though where I grew up in Tennessee, in the same climatic zone as Washington, the small, brownish-violet sweet 'Celeste' was said to be the hardiest.

I do not know of a trial of fig varieties in our climate, but a planting of thirty or so varieties would soon show which kinds are worth growing and which are not. As with many other plants, there is some confusion among fig varieties, and the mere fact that a gardener says he is growing a certain variety is no assurance that the name is correct.

Thomas Jefferson, whose extravagant passions in the plant world are both endearing and unreliable, went quite to pieces for 'White Marseilles'. At Monticello, Jefferson's house in Charlottesville, the 'White Marseilles' has been replanted after exhaustive efforts to make certain the name is correct.

Peter Hatch, the garden authority at Monticello, said that for the first winter or two the young fig trees were bent to the ground, wrapped, and covered with leaves. But more recently they have faced cold mountaintop winters with no more protection than leaves raked over their stems at ground level.

My plant of this variety came in a pot. It has had two growing seasons and is now eight feet high. I gave it no protection even as a small plant, though it grows against an east wall. This winter I shall give it a loose mulch of several bushels of oak leaves.

Both 'Celeste' and 'Brown Turkey' are fairly commonly sold and listed in nursery catalogues, and 'White Marseilles' is sold at Monticello, among other places.

Dormant plants, usually bare-root and roughly knee-high, or else in pots, are planted in March, before the new leaves come out. In England gardeners are always warned to restrict the root run of figs, but in our far more genial climate you simply plant the fig and do nothing else the rest of your life.

My friends in Arlington, who grow fine figs but are unsure of the correct names, have given me several cuttings. These should be about eight inches long, taken in fall after the leaves have dropped. They can be covered completely with sand and stored cold through the winter, then planted in pots in a sandy soil mix in February or March and planted outdoors around Labor Day and given some protection their first winter.

It is necessary for the cuttings to be planted with the tips above the soil. Usually the entire cutting, except for the top inch, is down in the earth, but that is not critical, and if half the cutting is aboveground there should be no problem. The three varieties mentioned here will fruit without pollination by insects, and a single tree will bear heavily without pollen from another fig.

Occasionally an ignorant writer will say the tiny fig wasp is necessary if fruit is to mature. That is not true of the varieties we grow here, but in some varieties it is necessary. The tiny wasp enters through the eye of the fruit, pollinates it inside, then leaves. We need not concern ourselves with the fig wasp, and in my view we have too many kinds of wasps in the garden already, and this may be the place to say that even if one is terrified of them (as I am) they should never be destroyed needlessly.

The old wild sweet violets of my childhood simply ran without supervision or care.

February

Roses Are Red, but Violets Are Bloomin' Lovely

PARMA VIOLETS, I always thought, were a bit sinister and decadent, and I feared I could not grow them. Every year or so I rev up and start to order some, then cross them off the final list. They are the inch-wide double fragrant violets on seven-inch stems that you never see — I have seen them only once in my life — but which were popular around 1900. They should be grown in cold frames, and as they do not like either much cold or much heat, they have never been popular with home gardeners. If the gardener is bold and brave, the two esteemed varieties are 'Marie Louise' and 'Duchesse de Parme'.

Much easier are the single sweet violets, though I have never grown them either. When I was a kid we had millions of purple violets toward the alley, and some were scentless while others were powerfully perfumed. I suppose the fragrant ones were *Viola odorata semperflorens,* as they started flowering in January and ran through April, then bloomed off and on again in the fall. Nowadays the best known of these single sweet violets is probably 'Czar', a rich purple, and 'White Czar', which is guess what.

This may be the place to say that our most common violet in Washington, as far as I can tell, is the so-called Confederate violet, *V.*

cucullata priceana, which is large, more or less flat-faced, white with bluish veins radiating from the throat. They are very showy but bloom only in early spring. They are scentless and are vicious weeds, but altogether desirable on rather steep banks. Once allowed in among flowers in beds, they take over, and their iron rhizomes are astonishingly hard to get rid of. Like many other violets, they produce masses of seed from cleistogamous flowers after the main blooming season. Those seed-bearing flowers have no petals, and the gardener never sees them, but the fat seedpods are borne near ground level. Either ants or the rains disperse them widely. It is a truly beautiful violet and admirable in the right place. It does well under garage eaves, by the way, or in many another waste space.

But back to the elegant sweet violets, varieties of *V. odorata.* There seem to be about a dozen varieties offered by nurseries nowadays. The 'Czars' are said to come true from seed and are supposed to be easy to grow. More highly esteemed at the height of the violet fever, say in 1910, were 'Princess of Wales' and 'Baronne Rothschild', both purple and large and powerful to the nose.

The well-known 'Governor Herrick' is not scented, so I cannot think why anyone would grow it, but perhaps its shortcoming would not be noticed in a bunch of the fragrant kinds.

All sweet violets like deep rich soil. Whenever I think of planting them — and some year I'll probably get around to them — I know where they should go, on the north side of a tall board fence, not hung over with trees but shielded on the east by another fence and on the west by a house. They would get strong light and ample sun in the summer, but no wind. I would space the young plants twelve by eighteen inches, having been warned for years against planting them too close together (as in such dandy books as *The Violet Book* of 1912). This site is raised some feet above an alley, so I would not worry about good drainage. But I would dig in about eight bushels of old — really black — horse manure and as much leaf mold as I could lay hands on, along with enough sand to make the bed somewhat gritty.

In England the gardener was always warned to give violets lots of sun, but here they would get plenty without the gardener's even trying, and you would not want them to bake all summer as they would certainly do if planted in an ordinary bed in the open.

In my own imaginary bed north of the fence, I might go so far as to collect a few scrap boards to make a rudimentary cold frame, to enjoy the flowers in perfection in the dead of winter. Otherwise, without the frame, they would bloom from October to Christmas and again after Valentine's Day.

These violets get leaf spot and red spider and probably other things, but I would not worry about it. I'd try three or six plants, giving them a good rich leaf-mold soil and ordinary care. The old wild sweet violets of my childhood simply ran about without supervision or care, and while the stems were quite short, they smelled as good as anything in the floral kingdom. So I would hope the showier kinds, like the princess and the duchess, would prove worthwhile without undue commotion over them. It is important, needless to say, to get varieties of *Viola odorata* if sweet violets are what you want. There are dozens or hundreds of other members of the genus that are pretty, and some are fragrant but most are not.

Sowing Seeds of Exotic Abandon

I THOUGHT IT WOULD BE NICE to suggest something for you that you don't have to do yet (as distinct from reminders that you should have done thus and so last fall) and something that will put you in mind of the lovely soft summer that is sure to come.

This charitable notion entered my mind as I was reading the Thompson & Morgan seed catalogue, one of the world's great compendiums of fantasy, and as usual I resolved anew to order some datura seeds. I did once, decades ago, and they were marvelous. But since I think of them every year and never get around to acquiring them, I thought this year I might mention them and let you raise them instead of me.

You know the jimsonweed (*Datura stramonium*), a vile, stinking, poisonous plant commonly found about city dumps and, I imagine, beneath gallows. The name is a corruption of Jamestown and is said to refer to the experience of a small troop of British sent to quell some disturbance at Jamestown, Virginia, in the seventeenth century. The soldiers either ate or smoked or otherwise incorporated into themselves some part of this jimsonweed and fell quite insane for eleven days. They then recovered and were as good as new, but they remembered the plant and named it for the site of their encounter with it.

It is said to be useful for witches. It can send you out of your head and (before all the swingy gardeners give it a go) out of this life. It can be lethal, as so many members of the nightshade family are. The only good thing I ever heard of the jimsonweed (apart from mention in a sort of handbook for witches, which spoke highly of its hallucinatory properties) is that it is almost totally resistant to disgusting things in the soil such as verticillium and fusarium and nematodes too, I think.

But not to go on about this worthless member of the datura tribe, I should warn you that Thompson & Morgan sells it for ninety cents a packet and speaks of masses of fragrant white trumpet-shaped blooms. And if you happen to know the plant for the stinking sticky thorny hostile poisonous creature that it truly is, you might lose faith in anything the catalogue says about other daturas. Which would be wrong, for a number of them are lovely in a coarse, exotic, abandoned sort of way.

Once I grew *Datura chlorantha,* which made chest-high plants of smooth (not fuzzy) rich green leaves amply hung with deep yellow double flowers, well perfumed, shaped like hanging trumpets. It did not show up well in the general garden picture, but I found myself going to admire it every day, as an unlikely flower indeed. And like daturas in general, it is as easy to grow as corn, requiring the same sort of sunny spot in nice ordinary good soil.

There is a no-man's-land in the datura tribe covered by the name *D. metel.* You are never sure exactly what *D. metel* will be. Usually it is a waist-high plant, wider than tall, with beautiful white trumpets that expand in late afternoon and breathe a scent very like that of tropical water lilies. It may be seen growing in rich soil on cotton plantations of the Mississippi delta, where it is an escaped exotic. People consider it a weed yet rarely chop it down because it is beautiful. Some of the trumpets are almost horizontal, others hang down. Some are white flushed with violet, others clear white, and in a seed catalogue's mixture, there may be flowers of deep purple and yellow and cream also.

All daturas are inherently coarse, with large leaves, usually hairy and weedy looking, so you need not expect anything like a lily of the valley or a sweet pea. Their beauty is more flamboyant, with the usual excitement that accompanies unembarrassed coarseness. I often think that daturas, tithonias (now there is another wonderful easy annual for you to try, and you just pick off the Mexican bean beetles, to save your asking later on), and tropical weeds of that sort were the original "If you got it, flaunt it."

But now we come to the treasure of the family, *D. suaveolens* (actually now called *Brugmansia suaveolens*), which is rather woody and grows to ten feet and, of course, is tender to cold. It is readily grown in a twelve-inch or larger pot. This is the plant called the angel's-trumpet. At a great Chelsea garden show in London a few years ago there was a Spanish courtyard garden paved with tiles, and through an iron gateway you looked down toward three white arches. Beneath the arches were great pots of this angel's-trumpet, and the effect was good enough to win a gold medal.

After blooming in late summer, these great plants may be trimmed pretty near the bone for bringing into the house for the winter, during which they are kept on the dry and cool side, then encouraged into lush growth the next spring and set out in mid-May.

The angel's-trumpet from seed grows along like the daturas, but is handsomest when trained to a single stem up to the height you want it, say six feet or so. You simply pinch out any side growth and give it a stick for support. When it reaches the desired height, you let it branch out at the top as much as it pleases. I am not really sure it will make all this growth and flower the first year, though I have read that it will.

I would sow the seed individually in a pot and try to keep it growing without check right through the summer. Start seeds in two-inch pots, shift them to four-inch pots, and then into twelve-inch pots or tubs. A little dehydrated cow manure and plenty of water and sun and heat will bring the plants on nicely and rapidly.

A final warning: if you have only shade, forget the daturas and brugmansias. They are sensible plants and, I believe, prefer sensible owners who love the sun.

Daffodil Delight

AMONG THE VARIOUS THINGS to drive a gardener crazy is the promise to tell somebody about a certain plant and then forget who it was.

"Did you ask about pig-lilies in Africa?" you may begin, with the person you thought had asked about them a month ago.

"No," they always say, looking at you as if a straitjacket were in order.

Be that as it may, somebody in Virginia did ask, most urgently, about the old double daffodil that you see sometimes in pastures, sometimes at the edge of hedgerows, sometimes along the shoulder of a farm road.

It could be the old 'Codlins and Cream' or the old 'Butter and Eggs', of course, or even the relatively modern 'Mary Copeland', which has a tough constitution, especially in the South.

But no. They described it all too well. Some years it does not bloom well, the buds open only partially. In other years it opens almost all the way but the petals never stretch out, and they remain green. In yet other years the buds open all the way, a rich tawny yellow, and in exceptional years these flowers are almost globular and distinctly on the large side. Usually the stems are no more than nine inches or so, but in exceptional years they may be twice that, or more.

This is almost certainly — I toss in the "almost" for modesty's sake

— the old double daffodil called 'van Sion', which first flowered in England about the year 1620. It reached America probably in the same century and is believed to be a daffodil mentioned in correspondence in 1730 between the Philadelphia botanist John Bartram and a friend in England.

It is, I believe, immortal; I never heard of anybody losing it once they had it in their garden, though Frank Galsworthy came close to losing his when some dense trees almost shaded it out. He crawled in there, rescued a few weak shoots, and in a few years found them well established once again in their new site in the sun.

Earth-moving machinery accounts for a good many of the daffodils along country roads and in old residential subdivisions in cities. I have several times seen the exquisite *Narcissus tenuior* in such places, and in parts of Virginia you see the old *Narcissus pseudonarcissus* where bulldozers have scooped them up and plopped them down.

But 'van Sion' owes its persistence primarily to a superb constitution. It evidently never gets basal rot. It does seed, though gardeners rarely notice the pods, and if these are scattered in a grassy place they often sprout to establish new colonies. I never knew it to seed in my former garden, where it had sat in fat clumps for half a century.

Daffodil buffs of today may find it hard to believe that as late as the 1930s this old daffodil was sold as a garden variety in seed stores, along with such other ancient creatures as 'Emperor' and 'Pheasant's Eye', though come to think of it the last-named sort is still sold.

I do not consider 'van Sion' worth growing in the garden, unless there is room for two hundred other sorts of daffodils and this old one is desired simply for sentiment's sake.

The seventeenth-century herbalist Parkison mentions in his wonderful book *The Paradisus* that

we first had it from Vincent Sion, borne in Flanders, dwelling on the Bank side (London) in his lives' time but now dead, an industrious and worthy lover of faire flowers who cherished it in his garden for many yeares, without bearing of any flowers until the yeare 1620; that having flowred with him (and hee not knowing of whom he had received it, nor having ever seene the like flower before) he sheweth it to Mr. John de Franqueville, of whom he supposed he had received it (for beyond the Sea he never received any) who findeth it to bee a kinde never seene or knowne to us before, caused him to respect it the more, as it is well worthy.

And Mr. George Wilmer of Stratford Bowe Esquire in his lives time having likewise received it of him (as did my selfe also) would needes appropriate it to himselfe, as if he were the first founder thereof, and call it by his owne name Wilmer's double daffodil, which since hath so continued.

But in the centuries since, the name Wilmer's Double Daffodil has virtually disappeared, and it is almost universally known as 'van Sion' in honor of old Vincent Sion, who has meanwhile sprouted a van to his name. The botanist Haworth named it 'Telamonius Plenus', by which name it is also well known. But in Tennessee and Virginia I never heard it called anything but 'van Sion'.

The flower resembles a fairly mad and electrified giant dandelion. It is said cattle never eat it, and of course rodents leave all narcissi alone, and I never knew the various hounds to eat it, though over the years they sampled a surprising assortment of flowers. Dogs, in my experience, tend to prefer white flowers such as gardenias and white water lilies. Not many dogs eat flowers, but if you raise the question at any good-sized gathering, you will be surprised to find that somebody or other has or had a mutt with a floral palate.

The old 'van Sion' has been used in quite recent years to breed double daffodils in New Zealand, I have read, and that most distinguished Irish breeder of white daffodils, the late Guy Wilson, while never using so outmoded a flower in his breeding, always kept a few clumps in his garden for memory's sake, and it was a rare year he did not comment on its blooming, usually about the first of April.

So much for this old flower. I imagine the next time I see the Virginia fellow who asked me about it he will reproach me for never letting him know. Eventually I shall certainly run into him and his wife again. I do not now remember which Virginians they were, but in the nature of things people always, without any exception, show up in due time, especially if you have failed to keep your promise to let them know about that daffodil or the pig-lily or whatnot.

Protect Us from Plants

WITH ALL MY TALK of peaches, figs, asparagus, and so forth, the gardener must not (and especially the gardeners' kids must not) suppose that nature is all nuts and berries for any noble savage to sample. Many plants are poisonous, and children should be taught to assume that all are, unless they are known to be safe.

I have myself sampled mistletoe berries without ill effect, yet they contain toxic substances. I have also eaten peach pits, yet the prussic acid in them can be fatal, and indeed they were used as a form of torture in Egypt. Also the yew berries (which birds eat) did me no harm, although they, as well as yew foliage (which is most dangerous), can prove fatal. The mere fact that birds or goats or some other animal may eat a plant does not mean it is safe for humans.

It is well known that the beautiful oleander is virulently poisonous. Armies in ancient times are said to have been decimated by roasting meat on oleander spits, as well as by eating honey collected by bees from *Rhododendron ponticum*. The oleander flower positively invites chewing, as the innocent honeysuckle does, and children must be warned specifically against eating flowers of any kind.

The lovely blue monkshood (*Aconitum napellus* and others) is fortunately rare in American gardens, since few plants are more lethal when eaten.

Older people forget sometimes that children will eat virtually anything. Modern kindergartens and children's stories may convey, quite wrongly, that plants are our dear little friends, as bunnies are. There is no need whatever to fly into an alarmed fit. We teach children not to sample gasoline, lye, furniture polish, and the restorative elixir that Aunt Emma takes when she is not feeling herself. It is merely necessary to add plants to the things not to be nibbled on.

The mere fact that sturdy tots, myself among them, have tried out mistletoe and yew without dropping dead means merely that I was perhaps lucky or perhaps did not eat enough. And yet plants like oleanders and aconites, even in small quantities, may prove fatal, so let us have no nonsense that because little Bobby reportedly ate thus and so without harm, it is safe for neighborhood kids to indulge freely.

It is said that water (even pure water) can kill children if several liters are drunk; it leaches out the body salts or something of the sort. All that is necessary, since the world is quite full of danger to exploring children, is to teach them not to explore hazardously, and this means not munching on twigs or berries or flowers they know nothing about.

One of the most charming accounts of poisonous plants I have seen — and the best for ordinary gardeners with a taste for the macabre — is a chapter in Brendan Lehane's *The Power of Plants*. Possibly the most wonderful nugget there is the news (or assertion — for surely it is not true?) that the mortality rate of the men of India dropped wonderfully once the custom began of killing the wife at her husband's death.

The ghastly implication, which I for one do not accept, is that women kill their husbands off like flies unless they know that when Old Tom goes, they go too.

But back to the garden. All fungi should be suspected of dire possibilities. One reads from time to time of "expert" gatherers of mushrooms who collected one too many. My mother was a great collector of mushrooms and had an utterly absurd test for deciding which ones were poisonous. It was only the grace of God that kept her alive. If I go to a house where they serve some wonderful mushroom delicacy collected by the host, I do not eat it.

Apart from fungi, of which I eat only the ones from the grocery store, and examine even them to make sure there is no oddball-looking one in the lot, there are plenty of poisonous garden plants. The lily of the valley contains heart poisons more potent, sometimes, than those of even the foxglove. The bracken fern (and I am deeply suspicious of all other ferns, too) contains strong poisons in all parts, especially the thick roots.

Stomach pains, convulsions, death, and so on result from eating yew, and the wilted foliage is particularly dangerous. Pasture animals from time to time are killed by eating it, though I think the main danger in gardens is that kids will be tempted by the exquisite soft fleshy gray-pink-scarlet berries.

The meadow saffron (*Colchicum autumnale* and others) is one of the finest full-blooming corms, like a giant crocus. From it is derived colchicine, which has uses in medicine, but the plant, if chewed on in the garden, may bring death from lung failure preceded by other dismal symptoms.

Columbines are supposed to be eaten by lions, who derive their courage thereby. I do not believe lions eat columbines. All parts of the plant are suspect, and children's deaths in remote places have been blamed on it. It seems one of the most demure and unoffending of flowers, but as you know in this world, you can't tell by looking.

The petals of the purple iris, treated with alum, made that exquisite green you see in illuminated manuscripts of the Middle Ages, but eaten plain they are said to be poisonous. I have eaten some in my day, but would not do so now. I have also chewed dried iris roots (I have heard that in Italy these roots are given to teething children) but see no need for this to become prevalent practice.

The Carolina jasmine is one of my favorite plants, being intensely fragrant, unlike the winter jasmine, which has no scent. The dangerous one is the Carolina native, *Gelsemium sempervirens,* and I have read that bees are poisoned by its honey. In any case its roots are even more dangerous. A drug used for migraine headaches comes from this plant, but children must not sample it, though often tempted, probably, since it resembles a particularly large and fine yellow honeysuckle.

There are any number of plants that look rather like parsley, carrots, or Queen Anne's lace, some of them extremely poisonous, others not. They should all be avoided in the wild.

The beautiful laburnum, that elegant small tree with flowers like yellow wisteria in spring, is said to have caused a number of deaths to children. The seeds are tempting. The one we grow in gardens is usually *L. wateri* (*L. vossii* is a synonym), which has few if any seeds and is therefore not so hazardous, but children must be warned against the plant in general. Like oven cleaner, it is fine if not swallowed.

Nero, he of the unsavory musical reputation, is believed to have killed Britannicus with a mixture of henbane, foxglove, and nightshade. Henbanes (*Hyoscyamus niger*) are said to grow in waste places, like jimsonweed, though I have never seen them there. They were great favorites with witches in former centuries. The late Margery Fish, a preeminent gardener of England, had the finest collection of henbanes in the kingdom. She had a fondness for plants overlooked by others but did not, of course, practice witchcraft. I have read elsewhere that henbanes are among the numerous plants producing hallucinations, if the dose is short of lethal.

Stick therefore to lettuce, turnips, onions, and collards. Friends to man.

Bright Spots in the Shade

❀ THE FIRST TIME I saw 'Frances Williams' with her great yellow-rimmed green ears I thought I had never seen a hosta so beautiful, and to this day it is a desirable variety, provided she doesn't get too much sun.

All hostas I know of flourish in moderate to moderately heavy shade. They like good leaf soil with some sand mixed in, but then they also do well in heavy clay loam. Like any other plant, they grow faster and more luxuriantly if given good soil — rotted black horse manure pleases them. They do not like to dry out, but in Washington I have never found it necessary to water them in summer.

There are relatively tall hostas, such as 'Krossa Regal', with upright leaves, giving the plant a vase outline; some of the blue-leaved forms, such as 'Blue Angel', 'Blue Umbrellas', and 'Big Daddy', make mounds of fine foliage three feet high.

No doubt the most prized hostas today are variegated kinds, and these may be quite large, as in 'Frances Williams', or quite low — useful for edging — such as 'Golden Tiara'.

A good many years ago a collection of hostas was exhibited at one of the big English shows, most of the plants from Japan, and I never got over the color photograph I saw of it. But this may be the place to point out the obvious, which so often needs pointing out, that showy hostas planted here and there at random can give an unsettling effect.

Many a gardener in the shade, when he first discovers hostas, has a heart too soon made glad and loses no time planting huge blue-leaved hostas edged with gold-leaved hostas next to large gold-leaved varieties (such as 'Piedmont Gold') edged with smaller green and white hostas (such as the old 'Thomas Hogg' or some of the newer, even more flashy white-splashed greens).

Within three years the result may be more dazzling than the gardener intended, but no great harm is done, as hostas are readily transplanted. A little discretion with the spading fork and the hostas can be redistributed to other parts of the garden with a gain in general calm.

Some of the large green-leaved forms, perhaps with blotches of different tones of green within the leaf (such as 'Antioch'), are exciting enough without going whole hog for more violent contrasts.

I am fond of tall flowers and therefore admire 'Tall Boy', which is not an esteemed variety today, but its plain green leaves sit beneath flower stalks five or six feet high bearing violet bells. Many gardeners would say the stalk is out of proportion to the mass of leaves, but if you want a plant with amazing stems, this is a good one.

You cannot be too careful to keep hostas out of strong sun. The site for roses or zinnias or corn is not at all right for hostas. I had a beautiful patch of the ancient *Hosta fortunei albopicta,* which despite its name is gorgeously acid green and yellow in the spring, later turning to solid green. Then a large nearby Norway maple finally died, much encouraged by me to the great trash pile in the sky, and to my chagrin the large old clumps of hostas died outright.

For gardeners cursed with shady gardens it is good to have at least one plant besides impatiens, which can be too showy.

Since mistakes can be so easily remedied by moving hostas about, the gardener should not be intimidated from trying kinds with gold or chartreuse or variegated leaves. And although I have seen at least one example of a garden with hostas in great variety planted cheek by jowl, the most pleasing result comes from planting them in moderation and avoiding violent contrasts. Plants of high drama like hostas may safely be allowed to just sit there without too much surrounding fireworks.

Good Sense Has Little to Do with Gardening

IT MAY BE TRUE that men like bigger flowers than women do. Whenever I have seen a dahlia a foot or more in diameter, I have been lost in admiration. It makes no difference that such flowers are not "useful" in a vase of blooms. Such a flower is like an elephant, a walrus, or a hippopotamus — marvelous in itself, apart from its usefulness as a watchdog or a pet.

Consider that wild dahlia from Central America, *D. imperialis.* Its flowers are small as dahlias go, about four inches, and the ray petals may hang forward a bit, giving a bell shape. But the amazing thing is height. This dahlia can reach thirty feet, and its great leaves, endlessly divided to produce an almost fernlike look, can be three feet.

It is one of those plants I have always wanted to grow, but of course you don't find it on every street corner. The sensible places to look for it are California nurseries, as this dahlia is sometimes grown there, more for its size than for the relatively slight beauty of its flowers, which are white or pinkish.

As I have never had a large garden, this dahlia would be a bizarre choice. It would make more sense to grow some of the four-foot bedding dahlias or the little eighteen-inch kinds that bloom like mad all summer.

But you don't garden and deal with gardeners for very long before you discover that good sense has little to do with it. A gardener with two flat acres of heavy clay loam baking in ninety-five-degree sunshine will suddenly realize that the perfect flowers are lewisias. The gardener with sea-dashed granite cliffs will conceive a passion for camellias or (soon afterward) bananas.

Long ago I learned there is no point arguing or pointing things out once a gardener gets an edelweiss in his bonnet. There is a fellow right here in this capital who is more or less sane and reasonable who has decided to line his wooden deck with bathtub-sized water tanks for fish and water lilies. But then (and how well I recognize that sudden light in the eyes when great thoughts hit like thunder) he has figured out that one side might as well be glass so he can see all the underwater activity while lounging on the deck.

I did once point out that there may be trifling problems bonding large sheets of glass to plastic tanks, and certain housekeeping details such as keeping the water clear enough that it's worth looking into from the side. Also, the glass will film over with algae and will need frequent scraping to keep it clear.

Never mind. That gentleman is far gone in his plans and will probably have the neighborhood flooded by the Fourth of July. Maybe it will work out as he dreams. Ha, ha.

As a kid I tried to graft a carnation to a prickly pear cactus, with the idea of improving the cactus flower. Fortunately I had nobody to teach me all the reasons why it could not work. I went ahead, I was excited, I was disappointed, and I got a million almost invisible spines in my fingers along the way. But then, we who suffer for science accept our lot.

People who understand nothing about gardeners assume the aim of the hobby (to use a meek word for what may become a fierce passion) is to have nice patches of colorful flowers all summer.

On the contrary, the aim may be to graft carnations to a cactus, or to see if a little aqueduct cannot be made from the stems of the imperial dahlia (as natives of Central America did). Or to be the only known creature in Washington who has a hedge of gardenias, and never mind the artifice involved in getting it through the winter.

For years I thought it would be well to have those great elephant ears you see in Louisiana, with the leaf blades pointing up, not hanging down. I now have some. For years I thought it desirable to have the ten-foot canna with nodding rose flowers (*C. iridiflora*), and now I grow it.

Who knows what the future holds? Will there be the tree dahlia for me yet? What about that honeysuckle from Burma, with waxy trumpets six inches long? As it makes a huge plant with leaves as big as a magnolia's, there might be some ingenuity required to keep it indoors in winter, but who doubts a gardener is ingenious?

The gardener's wife, who perhaps has argued against giant-flowered dahlias as unsuitable for the small garden, should not take premature comfort from the gardener's announcement that this year he is growing dahlias only four inches across. The little flowers may appear on a plant the size of a tree.

Wouldn't that be great?

That Growing Sense of Frustration

MY ONLY OBJECTION to the beautiful shrub *Kerria japonica* is that it suckers and overwhelms everything near it. It shoots up to eight feet and is hard to control.

But the fine gardener and writer the late Elizabeth Lawrence of Raleigh, North Carolina, has written that its only fault is that it is very fragile. With her it needed coddling, but with me it needs the attention of an ax.

Every gardener must have had the experience of hearing from some reputable and trustworthy gardener that a certain plant is miffy and uncertain, yet you have it all over the garden. Even more annoying is the comment that a certain plant is foolproof, yet you have utterly failed with it four times at least. The best any gardener can do is tell his own experience with a plant. If it grows like a weed he should say so.

Once I grew the blue dawn flower, *Ipomoea acuminata* (which was *Pharbitis learii* then), and gave a plant to a gardener who approached everything with an optimistic smile and who was in fact best known for having roller-skated across the state of Texas. This dawn flower, one of the most beautiful of all morning glories, though it is from Brazil and reputedly tender, I grew reasonably well on a half-shaded trellis. I mulched it for the winter, and it sprouted every spring and grew to eight or ten feet.

But my friend planted it on a south wall of his house, where it grew six ways to Sunday and moreover set seed, which it is not supposed to do, and self-sowed. Ordinarily this plant is treated as a greenhouse subject in Zone 7.

A beautiful summer climber, *Solanum jasminoides,* with little clusters of thumb-size white flowers from July on, has always been regarded as too tender to remain outdoors in winter. There is a blue form that is decidedly hardier, all the books say, and I have tried it twice but lost it to winter cold.

This solanum is not fully hardy in England, most of which lies in Zone 8, though it sometimes succeeds in London, as congested cities have more heat and less wind than the countryside. But here come Nancy Goodwinn and Douglas Ruhren of Montrose Nursery in Hillsborough, North Carolina, in colder Zone 7 to say it is "certainly" hardy in Zone 7. Generally this vine is thought to be risky north of subtropical Zone 9.

I bought two plants and left one outdoors and brought the other in for the winter. It will please me if the tender white form proves hardy where the best and hardiest of the blue forms, 'Glasnevin', proved tender.

Of course much depends on the plant's site — how much winter wind, how much early sun in January followed by afternoon freezing, and so forth.

Another plant common in subtropical regions is the crybaby tree, *Erythrina crista-galli.* This has gorgeous waxy scarlet clusters of large pea flowers. In Zone 7 it would never make a tree, but it will sometimes grow to six feet in the summer and bloom beautifully, then die to the ground in winter. I have known it to endure fifteen degrees below zero without harm, mainly because it had no living growth above ground in winter. If it were a tree with sap in its branches, it would probably die outright at eighteen degrees above zero. This particular plant had been brought from Samoa and had grown in a Zone 7 garden for decades.

A foolproof plant is the common larkspur. In theory you sow seeds in September where the plants are to bloom and they flower all spring or at least in May and June. But I have never succeeded with it. I let the larkspurs self-sow and a few do come up, usually within an inch of the main stem of a rose bush, where they cannot be allowed to stay. Sometimes a friend gives me young larkspur plants in March or April from her garden, where they self-sow heavily, and these make superb plants with me and bloom perfectly. But the next year I go begging again.

On the other hand there are various plants that have done quite well with me even though they are sometimes thought difficult to establish or to keep, such as *Clematis texensis* and *versicolor, Lilium lankongense* and *auratum,* and *Dasylirion texanum,* and some others.

To be defeated by the commonest of all petunias, the little white and pale lavender ones you sometimes see in alleys, is a humbling experience. Last year, as usual, these petunias, which I always grow from plants begged from a neighbor (for whom they come up from self-sowed seed by the thousand), again failed to seed themselves about at my place. As usual I got a few from the neighbor but was embarrassed to find a couple growing out of the stone sidewalk curb in front of my house. I can't keep them going in the garden, but they perpetuate themselves in the sidewalk. Life is neither reasonable nor fair.

Winter Has Sprung

❀ NOTHING IN THE YEAR is more hopeful, more exciting to the gardener, than the blazing sun of February and the lengthening days after the darkness of winter.

Technically, winter lasts another month, but every Washington gardener of this climate knows that spring begins sometime between February 4 and February 14. On the fourteenth the mockingbirds first sing, and even in chilly gardens the early crocuses have begun to flower, along with the snowdrops, which have been in bloom since January.

My first 'Yellow Mammoth', a crocus variety several centuries old, and I suppose the most common of all crocuses in gardens, bloomed February 11, or tried to. Its petals were torn off and left on the ground. I suspect sparrows. But once the full tide of large crocuses is upon us, I doubt any damage from birds will be noticed. The paper-white narcissi indoors are flowering, with one of the loveliest of all daffodil scents. The yellow paper-whites, the kind raised for the market by the millions on such islands as the Scillies and Jersey, are about to open. Their scent, which I keep trying to enjoy, is to me rather sickening.

With so much winter sunshine and such early springs, the gardener here has little incentive to force shrub branches into early bloom in the house. But such things as forsythia, kerria, quince, and star magnolia are easy if given a bucket of water and plenty of light and humidity (not direct sun) in a cool room, then transferred into vases as the blooms open. They are much appreciated by dwellers in apartments.

As the days lengthen, the cold strengthens, so goes the old adage, which means only that ice and snow are more likely after Christmas than before. But by this time of year we need not fear, even if there should be a first heavy snow or an ice storm in March. It will soon melt.

One year in this climatic zone (Zone 7), I was fit to be tied on March 23 when a heavy snow fell. I had camellia bushes about six feet high. The snow bent them and covered them so that part of the garden looked like a flat meadow covered with snow.

The camellias were in full bloom, and so were daffodils and some tulips and early fruit trees. My wife said that never before or since has she beheld me in such a temper. There were masses of white roses beginning early that year too. Fortunately the snow melted within a day and a half. The camellias stood up to six feet again, the daffodils and tulips emerged, and all the flowers were as fresh as if nothing had happened.

In another year there was a snow in Williamsburg on April 18, making fat caps of white on the late tulips. Again, it melted with no harm done.

Sometimes, especially during ice storms in March, much damage is done, but as there is nothing to be done about it, such things may as well be ignored.

One year, in ill-advised sarcasm, I answered in print an inquiry about what to do to protect spring-flowering bulbs from late ice damage. I said it was well to place little birthday candles among the flowers and keep them lit till the weather warmed. I was properly ashamed when I learned that some novices had tried to follow that advice. Gardeners do not care to be trifled with.

My friend B. is one of those gardeners who live in a forest in the suburbs but who has one little patch into which the summer sun streams fitfully. He therefore raises tomatoes every year, with what may be called indifferent success. I learn from his wife (for this kind of folly is never discussed man to man) that his tomato seedlings in the basement under fluorescent lights are already taller than they should be in May, when they should be planted outdoors. She and I secretly suspect his seedlings will be three to four feet high by then.

I well know the urge to get going with seedlings. I used to plant water lily seeds (tropical varieties) in January as a book advised. Nothing happened till late April, when they finally sprouted. Eventually I learned to spare myself several months of anxiety by planting the seeds in April.

It all depends. If you are a skilled gardener and have plenty of strong light and a cool room, you can start tomatoes in February. I have learned, however, that they do just as well (with much less agonizing on my part) if I plant them indoors in mid-March.

Our good cousins of Scotland are said never to be happy unless they are miserable, so I often suspect all gardeners derive from that kingdom. Few or no gardeners enjoy the spring (or winter) very much. They have flashes of ecstasy, but on most days they are worried about lilacs sprouting too early or magnolias getting frosted, or else they are suspicious of goings-on among the tree peonies that they fear are dead. Otherwise, why haven't the buds swollen? Things turn out all right, or at least they turn out as they will, and no matter how the gardener whines and bellows, one year is about as fine in the garden as the next.

In any case, you do not see gardeners giving up the garden until circumstances (not the weather) force them to live in apartments or in strange and dreadful places (climatically speaking) like Sioux Falls, Cameroon, or England.

This may be the moment — I am too embarrassed to say it in May — to mention that my friend Nick several years ago gave me a six-inch-high thing like a blackberry, which he said he collected from the garden of the late Mrs. Frederick Keays in Calvert County, and which he suspected was the 'Snow Bush' she often wrote about.

Later, when pressed hard, he admitted he had gotten it from the side of the road in some gravel, but it was (he said) the real thing.

I stuck it four inches from the alley fence, overhung somewhat by a large yew and flowering plum and other oddments. For some reason it just sat there for two or three years and was hard to see (one summer impossible to see) amid the little weeds (call them meadow grasses), but two years ago it rose into the light.

It now has flung itself about twelve feet into a sophora tree (which sprang up as a volunteer in recent years) and hangs its branches down like a weeping cherry. It is somewhat handsomer than a blackberry. Every spring I ask Nick if he thinks it might be a blackberry, and every year he flings his arms about more wildly, explaining in lengthy detail how it differs from, and is superior to, ordinary multiflora roses of the roadside.

When it blooms I agree with him, but I will not willingly give up phoning him in May to say I fear it definitely is a blackberry. That usually brings him huffing and puffing over, within four days, and I get the annual lecture.

It's a gardener thing.

To go from winter to summer you have to pass March.

March

Weathering Winter's Chill

MARCH IS A CHANCY TIME in the garden, with temperatures from severe freezing to summer heat, but of course to go from winter to summer you have to pass March.

It is particularly trying for plants not fully hardy that perhaps we have no business growing. My great agaves are no problem, apart from the misery of lugging them out in May and in in November. Only the least experienced or most optimistic gardener (same thing) is tempted to set them outdoors before May 10. I have done it earlier, and the leaves discolor and require some weeks to look right again.

If plants are to be grown through the winter in raised vessels outdoors, whether planter boxes, pots, or tubs, they should be ironclad hardy. I seem to have lost several plants in a large copper tub (verbena, delosperma, and salvia) that would have been safe if planted in an ordinary ground-level bed. Something to keep in mind next year.

A tantalizing plant is the night jasmine, which has the most intensely fragrant flowers I can think of. It is rather weedy and makes a shrub perhaps four feet high, with panicles of vaguely white, inconspicuous flowers from time to time in the summer months. Starting about late twilight or early darkness, the plant sends out waves of fragrance that can be smelled perhaps twenty feet away.

The main trouble, apart from the fact that it is by no means handsome to look at, is its tenderness to cold. Some gardeners in some places in some years manage to pull it through the winter outdoors, especially if it is backed by a south-facing wall and if wind is kept off the base of its stems and if the ground is mulched four inches deep. Treated thus, it begins to bloom in May and makes a much larger plant than a rooted cutting set out in May.

Last fall I dug up a four-foot-high, bushy night jasmine with a moderate ball of earth holding on to the roots and set it in a plastic trash bag, taking care to wrap it tight at the base of the plant, just above the earth ball. This was to keep it from drying out too much. In late January I gave it about a pint and a half of water and closed the bag firmly again. Unfortunately, the plant seems to be dead, somewhat like Monty Python's parrot, if you remember him, but shoots have come from the roots. While that is a good thing, the loss of the old thick stems means I shall have a smaller plant this year.

A friend here in town has a garden that is mostly subtropical, full of bamboos, bananas, clerodendrums, angel's-trumpets, and passionflowers. Virtually the entire garden has to go indoors in the fall. I offered to help him move stuff in, but he did not take me up on it. His big plants of angel's-trumpets, maybe six feet high, he simply plants out in spring as if they were a summer bedding plant. Then in fall he digs them with as much dirt on the roots as will hang on and lugs them to the basement, where he sets them in plastic tubs as large as he can find and afford. In other words, the same general method I use for the night jasmine. His plants, however, are in fine shape every spring when he plants them out; his angel's-trumpets do not die to the ground as my night jasmine does.

It probably works better to use big tubs than to wrap the root ball in a trash bag. And of course it is more dignified. He waters his dormant basement plants two or three times in winter, just enough to keep them from getting bone dry.

Any gardener doing these things the first time will be nervous and may experience disappointments, as I have with my night jasmine.

But eventually one gets the knack of it. It used to worry me awfully, how much water to give the agaves, and I find it hard to say even now what is best. It depends on the size of the plant and the pot, and whether it's kept in a warm room or a cool one. Water just enough to keep the thing alive. For several years now I have done it just right and almost by instinct with the agaves. I watered a bit too little and almost lost the night jasmine. It must be somewhat like making biscuits; it gets easy after a few times.

Correcting the Mistakes of Mother Nature

THE GREAT BLIZZARD dumped seven or eight inches on my garden, and I was out with a broom to knock the snow off my tall, narrow box bushes. The ten-foot box bushes are only about a foot thick and are supported by iron stakes (artfully concealed, if I do say so) for about four feet. Even so, they were bent to the ground and I worried, though not nearly as much as when I was younger and thought I must forever be busy to correct the mistakes of Mother Nature.

Now that the snow has melted, the bushes look as good as new.

The crocuses that were in bloom before the snow are still in bloom, a bit bedraggled, and I have not yet checked the thick clump of the daffodil 'Little Gem'. I am annoyed with it, anyway. It has flourished and increased like magic, but for many years the same variety in another part of the garden has just sat there and frequently failed to bloom in March.

So it seems unfair and wrong for this present three-year-old clump to be growing like a weed. Success in the garden is not always a pure pleasure.

I am never sure what to do, exactly, about certain plants that have been in the house all winter without water and that should go outdoors again in late April or early May.

Some things like bananas, cannas, elephant ears, and night jasmine have a distressing habit of sending up bright green new growth in February, even as they sit dry in their plastic trash bags awaiting spring. Ideally they should be potted up in tubs of rich soil and given high humidity and gradually increasing amounts of water. The trouble is I have no facilities for such goings-on. I want them to stay dormant until the end of April.

Every year, therefore, I muddle through, alarmed when the tender new growth dies back but afraid to encourage the new growth this early. Some years things work out better than in other years.

I much prefer the habits of crinums, those great lilylike flowers with leaves that flop on the ground, taking up much space. They are usually thought of as tender, but they are hardier than timid gardeners imagine.

In November the leaves start to die back, and soon there is a slimy mush and the gardener is greatly disturbed. For some years I fretted all winter that the crinums would rot in the miserable damp cold of January. I have not, however, lost any of the eight varieties I have tried, though after a winter of zero or near-zero temperatures some of them refuse to bloom. Which is their right.

But nowadays I don't worry about them at all and do not even mulch them. As the new leaves appear in April (a reassuring sight still, I admit) I give them an inch or so of rotted horse manure, and in the summer, if my energy holds out, I give them occasional extra watering.

Those who have not yet started seeds indoors are, on the whole, wise. Many a seedling from an early April sowing will fare better in the long run than those from earlier sowings.

Naturally, the gardener cannot be expected to learn from experience, and I see I have a few pots of infant tomatoes. Two years ago I saved seed of one of those heirloom varieties, and although tomato seed is supposed to be good for five years, I thought I had better plant a few to make sure they were viable. Germination was 100 percent. You could not expect me to just say, well, the seed is fine and throw out the test babies. So here I am with little plants that by May will be weak and stringy. As usual. But then I get superb yields, so whining is inappropriate.

The gardener should of course always plan ahead when starting seeds indoors. I have a friend who does this. He has bank upon bank of fluorescent lights, so he never runs out of space. As a result he raises about a thousand plants of assorted vegetables, all sturdy little fellows. He is rightly proud of them.

Everything goes well until the last of April (the seedlings having by then graduated to a cold frame) when it is time to plant them in the open garden. He then runs out of garden space and, more critically, out of time. One year he was so swamped he never got around to planting five hundred leeks, ordered from Georgia.

He has to feed himself and his wife, and he likes to take vegetables to his married daughter and granddaughter. Even so I sometimes question whether he needs one hundred or two hundred tomato plants. I am not sure he needs five hundred leeks, either, especially if they do not get planted.

But I treasure his friendship, partly because it is pure joy to behold him losing his mind every spring with tomatoes and peppers and onions and every other vegetable known to man jammed up in the cold frames. There are usually storms or bitter winds the day he plans to set things out, or else the temperature is in the nineties. The days pass and he races about.

Such friends cause one to think of oneself as positively sane. Or as near as never mind.

There Is Much to Be Done, We Must Get to It

THE QUICKEST WAY to spot a gardener — in case anybody, such as Sherlock Holmes, perhaps, should ever want to — is to ask about spring. Benighted folk think spring is when the peonies and roses bloom. Gardeners think spring is from late February to mid-April. Thus we see we are now in mid-spring and it is as usual splendid.

For a change I got out on a mild winter day and sheared back the barrenworts to the ground. This April, therefore, I shall enjoy fully the sheaves of pale yellow flowers, which if the old leaves are not fully cut back are lost in the tangle of old stems.

As you know, gardening involves thousands of little operations like this, and each one takes only a minute — thirty-two minutes to cut back the epimediums, actually — but as the years go by it is increasingly easy for the gardener to forget something. The day I sheared the epimediums was the day I should have pruned the grapes. I pruned some and shall now prune the others, and they will drip for several days. They will "bleed." The best thing the Department of Agriculture ever did was issue a report that this bleeding or dripping of grapevines pruned too late does no harm, and I think nobody would ever give it a thought except that it is called bleeding, and one therefore feels like a beast.

Daffodils opened ten days earlier than usual this year, the first ones coming March 4, and this may be the place to say that 'February Gold' and 'Peeping Tom' are of incalculable value for the gardener. Even in ordinary years when they open March 15 they are worth their weight in gold, though they are old varieties and as cheap as any and are sold in the fall in garden centers and numerous catalogues. If they were expensive or if you had to send to Vladivostok for them with import permits, I would still insist you acquire them, so it is nice that these truly first-rate garden flowers are easily available.

Which brings us to the question, why do you not have goodly patches of them? I speak here only to the slothful, since thoughtful sturdy gardeners already have plenty. Even three bulbs, planted a foot away from a box or a holly or a crimson-leaved nandina or a mahonia or any other nice evergreen, will have a pleasant effect, since even from three bulbs there will be six flowers the first year, a dozen the second year, and maybe twenty to forty the third year.

So often we wait till we have space or money enough for a grand display of some plant, but we would do better to get just the three bulbs, or even a single one, and get the show on the road. Otherwise, life goes by and we never get around to it.

I have always regarded the crocus as a mysterious flower, not in the sense of an orchid, but in the sense that I do not understand how the crocus behaves as the years go by. Such an innocent bold flower, without guile or disgusting ways (such as the delphinium has, rotting at the collar and that sort of thing), yet the crocus has several things up its sleeve, and comes and goes mysteriously.

In front near the sidewalk I once planted two or three hundred crocuses, and I smile now to think of the hours I pondered their selection. Is 'Lady Killer' too gaudy, too much of a good thing, do you think? Would 'Cream Beauty' on the whole be better? Well, I went on for days in my head and wound up with twenty-five or fifty bulbs of maybe ten varieties, and they were planted in small drifts, each kind separate, and for the next two or three years I complimented myself on the effect.

Then there came a spring in which a 'Golden Bunch' showed up among 'Blue Pearl'. And, to be brief, now you can hardly tell where the patch of 'Goldilocks' was, since some of them have died out, some of them have wandered elsewhere, and 'Violet Queen' has infiltrated into the original citadel of old Goldy.

This year, to my considerable pleasure and annoyance (in equal parts), I am alive with the big fat striped crocus 'Pickwick'. I do remember, dimly, that seven years ago I acquired twenty-five bulbs of this somewhat gross (and like all crocuses, irresistible) variety, but there were so few the next spring that I thought something must have been wrong with the corms, though they looked healthy enough when I planted them. As in so many other cases, I did not worry foolishly but thought win some, lose some, and went on to higher things than my own disappointment.

Each spring a few 'Pickwick' show up, not necessarily where I remember planting them, and some of them have showed up in places where, I can swear in any court on any Bible, I positively did not plant them. But this has been a very minor mystery, a few odd ones showing up every spring. This year huge blooms of the striped giant have turned up among my delicate small crocuses. I do not think they have seeded. I think the squirrels, on their endless rounds of whatever squirrels do, have inadvertently transported tiny cormlets, and these in two or three years of growing along have built up their strength and are now flowering.

Crocus tomasinianus, on the other hand, the most notorious of all crocuses for seeding itself about, has never seeded itself at all with me. I suspect I have a hybrid, and a sterile one at that, since the true wild variety seeds everywhere.

When other gardeners tell me of similar mysteries I am aware that gardeners, as a class, have very poor memories and probably just forgot where they planted something. I too keep forgetting where I planted something. Only last year I moved the great ligularia 'Desdemona' to a better site and forgot it, and only after several months realized that all of a sudden 'Desdemona' was missing. She is nowhere to be found. It is incredible, in a place as small as mine and given my enormous fondness for the plant, that it could be misplaced. Possibly some criminal stole it. That is the best thing to think if you are missing a plant.

I have known cases in which somebody stole something like 'Desdemona' and then, in a cowardly way and probably in the dead of night, sneaked back into the garden and put it back in some strange place.

The Growing Anticipation of Spring

❀ THE DAY BEFORE THE COLD and snow began I planted two clematis, knowing snow was predicted. As always, when you find clematis at this time of year in cartons, the plants had already sprouted, and that soft growth will be killed. The alternative is to plant it in a pot, keeping it cool and damp until mid-April, but when I have done that in the past I have neglected the pots and only got the plants set out months later.

One thing a novice may not know is that the clematis roots, which are like leather shoelaces, are rammed into the little pots and packed with peat to keep them moist. That is good. But when planted in the garden (in a one-cubic-foot hole, with plenty of leaf mold) the roots should be dusted free of the stuff in the little pot and spread out, and the crown of the plant (where the stem joins the roots) set a full two inches below soil level.

Another thing not obvious to gardeners the first time a clematis is planted is that the stem is quite delicate and brittle where it joins the roots and is easily broken off. Use care when unpotting and never hold the plant by its stem but by its roots.

Even if the top is killed, new growth will rise from below ground, and by the third year the stems will be like modest ropes and the plant will cover a space the size of a door.

With terrible weather I congratulate myself anew (a thing gardeners do more than is good for us) that all through the warm or even hot days I did not remove the plastic wrapped around those few roses that are tender to cold wind, the teas. Hybrid teas and floribundas are better off without protection, probably, but the nineteenth-century teas can be lost in sudden freezes.

When I say wrapped, I don't mean the rose stems are wrapped like so many umbrellas or water pipes. The wrapping is a good six inches away from the trunk or main stem, the space is lightly filled with twigs of fir or cedar, and the top is completely open to sleet or anything else that falls.

This protection, slight as it is, will do the trick. My tea roses are on their own roots; that is, they are not budded on an understock, so even if they are killed to the ground they will grow again (it says here) from the roots.

One surprise this year has been the daffodil 'Little Gem', a yellow trumpet on a stem five inches high. I have grown it for twenty years or so, and after the first year it starts to peter out or at least to bloom fitfully. Once my old clump stopped blooming for three years, and I said farewell to the feeble tufts of leaves, but the following spring it bloomed like mad. Clearly the tiny bulbs had divided and needed a while to build up to blooming size. Unlike humans, plants do not go in much for sex (flowers) when in feeble health.

But back to the nice surprise. A couple of years ago I planted another clump of this daffodil in a sunny bed in which tomatoes grow in summer. They bloomed the first spring, and then this second spring they tripled the number of flowers. It has occurred to me that they like the fat soil and full sun of their site far better than the refined woodland leaf-mold site in which I had always grown this variety.

I am sure more damage is done in clumsy inappropriate efforts to save plants, or their new leaves, in late freezes than is done by the freeze. One exception I make is for young tree peonies. They have an annoying habit of starting to leaf out in February though they bloom in April, and the flower buds are exposed far too early in some years. This year I have an upturned bean basket over *Paeonia moutan,* the wild single white-with-dark-central-blotch species from western China and Tibet.

I had it in a perfect place in front of a yew tree, but the yew tree, which has greedy, fierce roots, began to get the better of it, so I moved it last fall to a better spot. It has never bloomed and is still only a foot high, but this year I see what look like flower buds. It would be nice before I die to see the thing bloom. The fat Japanese doubles bloom well every year.

Coming Attractions

WHEN YOU ORDER PLANTS by mail you soon notice that they arrive at the least convenient times.

On April 5, for example, the temperature may be twenty or eighty-five degrees. The earth may be parched or it may be under snow, hail, or flood. That is when my first batch of plants is supposed to arrive, and whatever the weather I'll be delighted to get them.

As far as money and energy hold out, I like to try plants new to me or replace old favorites that have long since gone to the great compost pile in the sky.

Among the treasures are these:

Solanum dulcamara variegata. Every gardener in temperate zones knows the black nightshade, a somewhat weedy vine with lavender potato-like flowers followed by red poisonous berries in small clusters. It is a troublesome weed if not controlled, as it thrives in heavy clay loam, sun, and our splendid warm summers. But this variant has white leaves with a green central blotch. It probably is not as vigorous as the basic kind — most variegated plant forms are not.

Ampelopsis brevipedunculata elegans. This is the green-and-white-blotched form of the porcelain berry. Like many variegated plants, it reverts to plain green, and if the green form is not cut away it will soon overwhelm the white-and-green leaves. The plain green form is altogether beautiful, but in Washington it is a vicious weed and needs careful watching; not only will it happily smother any plant in its way (if you can imagine it, I lost a five-year-old white wisteria vine this way), but also birds eat the berries (of a beautiful turquoise color peppered with black dots), and the seeds come up everywhere. This form is not so vigorous, but all members of the family should be under the gardener's eye.

Anthemis cupaniana. For some reason this daisy is uncommon, and I have looked for it for several years. It is much like ordinary yellow marguerites, which themselves are among the most satisfactory perennials here, blooming off and on for much of the summer. This one has white daisies about two inches wide or so in quantity above silvery leaves. It grows to only a foot or so but often weaves itself up other plants to greater heights. I am trying it beneath tea roses.

Two boltonias are now popular, 'Snowbank' and 'Pink Beauty'. It is often said that the pink one is washed out and ugly, but I have many times seen it looking handsome and desirable. Both have inch-wide aster-type flowers on stems perhaps four feet high, and the main thing is they bloom in very late summer. A bit weedy, so for years I resisted them but have now succumbed.

The pinks and dianthus are shaky propositions in Washington, as many of them do not like muggy summer nights and none of them likes heavy clay. Still, if you work in some sand and leaf mold, many of them will do. I am trying two old kinds, 'Charles Musgrave' and 'Mrs. Sinkins'. The lady splits her calyxes and therefore is a bit raggedy in flower, but well scented. We shall see. Maybe they will settle in beneath the rose bushes.

Melissa 'All-Gold'. To my surprise, this gold-leaved variant of lemon balm does not care to be baked in summer but evidently likes a bit of shade and dampness, just as the green form does. I had one in a whiskey barrel and kept it watered, but in a hot dry spell it died in a matter of three days. Now I know better.

Gaura lindheimeri. This is one of those somewhat plain perennials that have become fashionable. It has small pinkish white flowers up and down its four-foot stems and has a long summer season.

Salvia uliginosa. This is one of the most beautiful of blue sages, with sky-blue flowers along its five-foot stems. It is what I call a wobbly, that is, a plant that usually needs staking, though I have seen it in glory here unstaked. Salvias are hard to stake without the stakes being obtrusive, but one muddles through. The name suggests it should grow in a swamp, but I have seen it in an ordinary border. It is on the very edge of hardiness, and if it is not protected in winter, you may lose it.

Clematis integrifolia 'Olgae'. Why this clump-forming clematis is so rarely seen in gardens I cannot say. Perhaps it is one of those plants that when you see it, with its nodding pullet-egg-size blue or pink flowers, you admire it greatly but never order it. That has been my case, a shortcoming I hope to correct this spring.

Viola labradorica. This is a violet from the far north with rather ordinary flowers, but the leaves are somewhat purplish, so it is distinctive. Sometimes violets settle right in and seed themselves everywhere, or they may just sit there for some years, and again they die on July 17.

Support for the Red, Round, and Ripe

❀ A FEW WORDS about tomatoes. In the garden, where space is priceless, tomatoes can be set as close as a foot apart, provided the soil is rich and watering is tended to every day or so, and provided the plants are grown to a stake six feet above ground. In such an artificial system, the plants are kept to a single stem by pinching out the side shoots and tying the main stem to the stake every foot or so.

Tomatoes can also be grown in pots and tubs, but do not expect a regular main-season tomato with large fruit to do its best in less than two and a half bushels (eighty quarts) of earth.

Some tomatoes are better suited to containers than others. 'Super Bush' grows to only three feet and could be tried in a whiskey barrel or even a five-gallon pail. Some varieties (edible, but grown mainly for ornament) can be grown in flower pots six to twelve inches in diameter.

But in the usual outdoor city garden, tomatoes should be planted at least twenty inches apart, and results will be better if each plant is given four square feet (twenty-four by twenty-four inches) of soil surface.

The point is that if you cannot manage ideal conditions, just do the best you can, as Nancy Reagan used to say, and of course be satisfied with such slight success as you achieve.

The usual support for tomato plants in the garden is the wire cage. Usually this is made of steel reinforcing wire, the mesh five or six inches square. The cage should be twenty-four inches in diameter and five or six feet tall. You just bend it into a cylinder; it is easy enough.

The great disadvantage comes in storing these cylinders over the winter. They are no problem if you have space in a shed or garage to stand them up, but even then they are a nuisance to lug in and out. Instead of the cage, you can make a tepee of three wooden stakes (or trimmed branches) seven or eight feet long and stuck into the ground a foot or so. Or you can use posts with wire or mesh strung between.

Remember that you have to reach in to gather the tomatoes, so do not use a trellis against the garage, say, without thinking how to gather the fruit.

I have never grown one of the ultra-vigorous varieties such as the old 'Triple-Crop', but if the plant is given a barrel-sized hole filled with rich rotted manure, leaf mold, and fine loam earth and is watered two or three times a week, the plant will grow ten feet or more. It would be pleasant over an arbor or against a wall, but needless to say it would have to be tied to supports.

Tomatoes can also be allowed to sprawl on the ground without any support at all. A mulch would help keep the fruit clean and away from the damp earth. I have grown tomatoes this way with reasonable success, but you need plenty of space. Four feet apart is not too much to allow. Also slugs, Carolina tortoises (if you are lucky enough to have them), squirrels, birds, and (gasp) rats will attack the fruit, so you need to grow extra plants to make up for faunal assaults.

All tomatoes should be picked when dead ripe and eaten that day. They should not be put in the icebox if you want the best flavor. But it often happens that various beasts wait until the fruit is utterly ripe before descending on it. You may therefore find yourself picking the tomatoes when they are red but not dead ripe. Sometimes you may pick them when they are only orange for some reason. Let them ripen on a cool or room-temperature shelf out of the sun. Most gardeners are determined to set them on sunny windowsills, but out of the sun is better.

You may also resort to protective nets. These are usually black plastic with mesh about an inch square, and they should cover the entire plant. Squirrels will not likely go under the nets at ground level, so you can usually get away with not netting all the way to the ground. You may wonder why squirrels do not simply chew through the nets, which they could easily do. Fortunately they do not. Or not yet.

If tomato plants wilt from fungus disease, there is nothing to be done except get rid of the plant, and not on the compost pile. Fortunately most varieties today are resistant to disease.

Several insects attack tomatoes, but I have never sprayed my plants and have never had trouble. Sometimes the handsome and fierce-looking, finger-thick green tomato hornworm may appear. I dislike killing them. Perhaps a few tomato plants could be grown separately and the hornworms transferred to expendable plants elsewhere. Not your neighbors', of course.

Despite what some books say, tomatoes can be grown in the same spot for years as a rule, but if disease appears you will know you should have given them a new location. Thus it is sensible to give them a new site every couple of years if possible. If not possible, keep planting them in the same place and hope for the best, for usually all will be well.

Books often say the plants should receive an inch of water a week. I find that they do better with considerably more water than that. A good soaking every other day has worked well with me. If several shovelfuls of rotted manure have been dug into the planting site for each tomato, no additional fertilizer is necessary all summer. But use your brain. If the plant is not growing vigorously, give it fertilizer and water no matter what some book says. I have often read that tomatoes will be better flavored if they don't get too much water, and I suppose it depends on what is meant by too much.

Mine have been best when watered heavily. I like them to grow to eight feet or so and to look like a tropical jungle. I have not noticed any shortage of fruit or loss of flavor when grown as luxuriantly as I can manage.

Usually a seed packet says how many days are required before ripe tomatoes may be expected. Depending on variety, it may be sixty-two days or seventy or ninety. That is from the date (usually May 5) that the young plants are set out. If there is less than full sun (a bit of shade from a nearby tree), additional days will be needed. If there is cloudy weather, additional days will be needed. So do not count on an exact day to harvest your fruit. It may be sooner or later than the seed packet says.

There are many varieties grown only for the market, and there is no point growing them. Their market virtues of hard, firm flesh are vices in the home garden. You want soft, juicy tomatoes, too delicate to put on a truck and ship five hundred miles away. Stick to varieties recommended for the home garden. Admittedly, some commercial varieties ('Rutgers' is a famous example) are also excellent in the home garden.

There are determinate tomato plants that grow to a certain size and then stop, bearing fruit but not growing new branches with additional fruit. 'Celebrity' is perhaps the most famous example. It should be grown in cages, and although the plant stops growing, its fruit is borne over a good long season.

But most tomato varieties of consequence are indeterminate plants; that is, the plant keeps growing, blooming, and setting fruit until cold weather stops it. 'Better Boy' is typical and is, I think, now the standard good garden variety in favorable climates such as that of Washington.

Do not be afraid, however, if you have never grown tomatoes. Just go ahead, and you will have fewer disasters than you expect. Once I grew a wretched golf ball–sized thing called 'Copiah' and was happy with it. It is common to have splendid success, and I think the usual cause for failure is lack of an open, sunny site.

Sometimes I think too much is made of differences in flavor. All home garden varieties I have tried have been excellent when picked ripe (and there is no reason to pick them until then). I have read that 'Celebrity', for example, is not of the highest quality, but I have eaten this variety (grown by a neighbor) and found it as good as varieties said to be more flavorful. Also I have eaten both 'Brandywine' and 'Red Brandywine' (totally different kinds, but each is sometimes said to be the ultimate tomato), without noticing they were any better than 'Better Boy', to give an example.

Mind you, I may lack the connoisseur's palate, but it may be that with tomatoes (as with almost everything else in America) there is a good bit of blathering nonsense and propaganda going on, and relatively little experienced and impartial judgment.

Right at the Start

SOMETIMES I HAVE BEEN entirely too enthusiastic in steril-izing soil. When starting seeds indoors for transplanting later to the garden, you want to prevent damping off of the infant seedlings. If the soil is not sterile, the seedlings are likely to collapse and die.

On the market there are various packaged mixes that are supposed to be sterile, and seeds may be sown directly into such products, taking care that the pot or flat is clean.

But sometimes the gardener prefers to produce his own sterile soil rather than buying it. Do not make my mistake of putting garden soil in a large pan, covering it with water, and boiling the bejabbers out of it. This will indeed sterilize the soil but will oversterilize it. Without going into the matter further, take my word for it that this is not the way to sterilize soil.

Instead, take your regular good loam, put it in something like a roasting pan, and bake it in the oven at 275 degrees for half an hour. Let it cool, fill your pots or flats, and sow the seed.

Another way is to take the seed from the packet and sow, not in the sterilized soil that you have prepared, but in milled sphagnum moss or vermiculite. Watch carefully, and keep the seeds damp but not wet. When seeds sprout (within a week or less if you are growing tomatoes) remove the sprouted seeds twenty-four hours after germination. This will seem odd if you have never done it. The tiny stem will be less than half an inch long, and the tiny pair of first leaves (the cotyledon) will be closed flat together.

Plant the little creature in your prepared sterilized soil. You can use a pencil or some such instrument to make a hole in the soil into which you drop the seedling. You do not want to injure the tiny roots. Gently firm the soil around the baby plant, water it, and give plenty of light, either under fluorescent lights or on a quite sunny windowsill.

You should now have no problem with damping off or cutworms or any other misery. Simply let the little plant grow, aiming to produce a sturdy little fellow six inches tall by May 5, when you transplant it to the garden.

If you can buy young plants from a garden center or hardware store at a reasonable price just when the time arrives for planting outdoors, you may save yourself the trouble of raising them yourself.

But, as an example, I want some plants of *Nicotiana langsdorffii,* a tobacco plant with green flowers, and *Mirabilis longiflora,* a four-o'clock with long quill-like white flowers. Neither one is going to be available at the garden centers I deal with, so my only recourse is to raise them myself.

However, if you want half a dozen plants of some popular variety of tomato, you may think it easier and about as cheap in the long run to buy the plants ready to set out. But even so, if you are properly organized and set up at home (and do not suddenly take off to London for a week) you will find it much cheaper to buy a packet of seed and raise your own plants for the next four or five years.

As with so much in life it's a trade-off between convenience and dollars.

This may be the place to mention that those nicotiana seeds (and petunias also) are sown on the surface of the soil, not buried a quarter-inch deep. They need light to sprout. That is why petunias often appear from last year's plants in the open garden — seeds fell on the ground in November and sprouted in April without anybody's touching them, while petunia seed planted indoors and covered with soil will never sprout.

Another thing — those wildflower seeds that people plant in mixtures are often a disappointment. You will get no results at all if you simply sprinkle them on a grassy patch or on an old flower bed with weeds here and there.

The wildflower seeds should be sown on soil that has been dug and brought to reasonable tilth. Then they will sprout. Many of them are perennials and will not bloom the first year, but they should the second.

In any case, do not expect a packet of such seed to provide you with a fine assortment of wildflowers for years to come. Most will die out, and the process must be done again.

Speaking of wildflowers or weeds, I marvel that the sky-blue chicory, so often seen on roadsides or in alleys, is not more often brought into the garden. The color is irreproachable, and the plant is as tough as dandelions. It is a great comfort to those who want a flowery meadow but who have been disillusioned in their attempts to create one.

Spring is the time of a thousand tasks.

April

Spring Is the Time of a Thousand Tasks

IN SPRING CLEANUPS the gardener often finds that a shrub or small tree needs to be moved to a site that will give it more room, and while late April is not the right time to do the job (try October or late February), it's better to do it now than not to do it at all.

This past week I moved a climbing rose about six feet high, getting it into a prepared spot so it was not out of the ground more than five minutes, and it has not wilted a leaf, even though the leaves were fully out when it was dug. The critical thing is water. This plant will need careful watering, not only at moving time but through its first summer.

Last fall I moved (or assisted with the job, which was done mainly by Mr. H., who is an enthusiast of trees) what was thought to be a ten-foot *Magnolia stellata*. Magnolias are touchy in the roots and dislike being trifled with, and spring, not fall, is the safest time if they must be heaved forth.

To my delight the magnolia took no offense and has been blooming its head off. It is not the star magnolia, however. As its buds showed color I assumed it was *Magnolia liliflora nigra*, especially as it has a narrow upright shape, but now it is clearly a good deep rose variety of *M. soulangiana*. Rose is a rich and rare color at daffodil time.

Some years ago a camellia fancier, the late Philip Amram, gave me a couple of sprouted seeds. I thought it was foolish to plant them, as it can take ten years from seed for a camellia bush to get to forty inches and to start blooming well. But this year the bush is loaded with deep rose semidouble flowers, as handsome as a camellia ever needs to be. A word of warning or encouragement: if you grow camellias or peonies (or many other plants) from seed, do not judge them at their first or second blooming.

The first year this camellia bloomed it had shabby flowers, small and almost single. The second year it looked better, and this year it is good enough for any Mobile beauty to wear in her hair.

The same has proved true of a regular Chinese peony grown from seed. It sprouted beneath a fine old plant of the red-flecked white 'Festiva Maxima', and I moved it when it had only baby leaves. The first year it bloomed (and it took a dozen years because I neglected it and it had to fend for itself) I thought it was possibly the only ugly peony I had ever seen. But a couple years later it produced presentable flowers, double and a sort of mulberry color.

Needless to say, the gardener commonly has no idea of the parentage of camellias, irises, roses, and peonies that he raises. One of my favorite roses is one from seed, and my records show that its parents were 'Madame Grégoire Staechelin' pollinated by 'Dortmund'. The resulting rose from this supposed parentage is cluster-flowered, pink with lighter centers, each flower about an inch across, and scented of musk. While the parentage of garden roses is highly complex, so that almost anything may come from a cross, still this seedling rose is so utterly different in so many respects from its parents that I assume I am wrong about them. It looks as if it might be a seedling of the hybrid musk 'Kathleen', which I used to grow (and would grow still except a concrete mixer drove over it).

My old plant of guinea-hen flower, *Fritillaria meleagris*, which country people called toad lily, is in bloom again, with four somber red-violet checkered blooms on its two stems. For almost twenty years it has sat there behind an encroaching shrub of Korean box (which I do not like — one of my few indulgences in impulse buying a few years ago), and I cannot imagine why it is happy just where it is. It is the sole survivor of fifty bulbs.

This is the precise moment to move snowdrops, while they are in full mature leaf and before they begin to die down. I have a few that have been overgrown by some Kurume azaleas. Every year I vow to get under there and move them forward, but spring is the time of a thousand tasks and one task (I have been reading Sir Richard Burton again), so I hope this year the job will finally get done. They move nicely when dug with the earth still attached to their roots. They are not dried off but are planted instantly — do not answer the phone — and watered well. They will bloom in their new spot next February as if they had grown there for years.

Dalliances with the Dahlia

DAHLIAS ARE THE SHOWIEST creatures of the late-summer garden, and I shall say how I have grown them, off and on, since youth. I go by the 1951 recommendations of Stuart Ogg, a dahlia personage to be reckoned with.

But first, it's true that if you get packaged dahlia roots at a hardware store and plant them six inches deep outdoors anytime from now on they will emerge in a few weeks (even if it's cold and rainy, even if there's a light snow) and bloom well.

But that is not a very elegant procedure. It is better to wash the roots, set them in a shallow cardboard box in a window where they get sun. Then, when the shoots begin to sprout, you can plant them out, in full sun. The greatest enemy of dahlias is shade, tree drip, and (when planted in sun as they should be) lack of water in July and August.

Still better than the bare roots in the box is to start them in a shallow box of damp peat moss (not dry, not wet, but just damp enough to hold together briefly when you squeeze a handful).

The shoots will emerge within the week usually. When these

shoots are three inches long, cut them off with a sharp knife. There will be three sets of infant leaves. Cut just at the base of the leaves nearest the tuberous root. Plant each one in a three-inch pot filled with one half peat moss, one quarter sand, and one quarter good garden loam. (I have rooted them in water and in plain dirt, and once I rooted a broken-off shoot only a bit over an inch long, but you may as well use a sensible mixture.)

With temperatures in the sixties, they root easily indoors and do not need bottom heat. In theory the pots should be placed in a covered empty aquarium or else in a plastic-bag tent, opened to the air at night. One danger is condensation in a closed glass or plastic environment with subsequent rotting of the cuttings. In practice, I find they root perfectly well without glass or plastic.

When they are rooted, as shown by new growth, you shift each cutting to a five- or six-inch pot and grow them on till the middle of May, when they should be somewhat bushy, with three or four sets of leaves. Then you plant them outdoors next to a wooden stake. The stakes may be three-quarters or one inch thick, or even thicker if you have some on hand, and should reach above the ground a good three and a half feet.

After the young plants have been set out, pinch out the growing terminal bud. As the plants grow, you may pinch out the end leaf buds of the strong side shoots. Keep the ground weeded, and as hot weather arrives, keep the plants watered. Use twine to tie them every eighteen inches to the stakes.

We do not have terrible gales in late summer as a rule, but even so the dahlias need to be staked, and the stake should be set in place immediately before setting out the plants; otherwise it is easy to damage the roots by driving the stake in later. By mid-July it is well to mulch the plants with two or three inches of whatever you use for mulch, but do not mulch right up to the stem. Leave six or eight inches bare.

There are various bugs and diseases of dahlias, which I do not bother with. I consider spraying a nuisance at best and a hazard at worst, and my dahlias did well enough. A surface dressing of old manure in June is good, but since few people have that, any ordinary chemical fertilizer (5-10-5 or 5-10-10, for instance) is all right. A handful per plant, scratched into damp soil ten inches out from the stem, then watered thoroughly.

Mr. Ogg used to water his dahlias six hours at a time, once a week, but that means little as I do not know how hard the hose was running. A good soaking once a week is about right. A shortage of water, rather than a shortage of fertilizer, is the usual cause of scrawny dahlia flowers.

Dahlia flowers come in sizes from an inch and a half (small pom-pons) to things more than a foot across. The huge ones are, of course, gross and vulgar and irresistible. They require frequent nipping out of the developing flower buds, leaving perhaps four per plant.

More reasonable for the garden are the small decoratives and small cactus types (four to six inches in diameter), as many more flowers per plant are produced. Fans of the dahlia often join local dahlia societies where (as in all floral societies) members boast and whine agreeably together and compare notes and explain what went wrong just at the time of the dahlia show.

Colors run from white through pale mauve to rich purple, red, yellow, and orange, and some have two colors, such as red with white tips to the petals. Think of yourself as growing corn when you grow dahlias. They like good deep soil. Give them the sort of spot you would give your best roses, irises, or zinnias. Planting them in a bosky dell (where you would plant azaleas) is certain to bring total disappointment.

If you make cuttings as I have outlined, you should get four or five plants from one tangle of roots, and these plants from cuttings will make as large a plant as if you had planted the whole clump of roots. This I doubted until some years ago, when I made one cutting, then planted the rest of the root clump intact. There was no difference in quality or quantity of flower.

The dahlias are dug up at the end of October with some dirt on the roots and dried for a few days, then turned upside down (the stem has been cut off an inch or so from above the roots) so no moisture remains in the stem. They are stored dry (but not bare) in peat in the basement or some such place. They are brought out in March or April and the process started again. Some of them rot or wither during winter. Pay no attention to it. You will have plenty if you make cuttings.

If you are much alarmed at raising cuttings and plant the entire root clump just as bought at the store, do not let more than four or five of the shoots grow. When they finally reach the surface, there may be more; simply pinch off all but a few (every one of which would have made a nice plant if you had followed the rooted-cutting procedure).

Facing Up to the Cold Facts

❀ FREEZES, WHICH MAY OCCUR well into April in Zone 7, are not the terrors new gardeners often consider them to be. I have said this before, but gardeners are a nervous lot and need to be reassured repeatedly.

In the first place there's not much you can do about a freeze, and in the second place such early flowers as daffodils, anemones, scillas, wild tulips, and so on are quite used to them. In rare cases (as in repeated late freezes) the flower may be damaged, but usually no great harm is done.

People who cannot tolerate the anxiety of possible damage to, say, early magnolia flowers should simply not grow them. Normal gardeners, on the other hand, soon learn to take the weather in stride. They know that if you refuse to plant anything that may be damaged by weather you will not have anything at all.

Freezes are by no means the only hazards. There are also torrential downpours (usually scheduled at the height of the peony season), unbelievable droughts, tornadic winds, and, I suppose, sooner or later earthquakes, all of which may damage a plant.

There is no need to phone about the city in the middle of the night every time a change of the weather occurs. Come on now, you are supposed to be tough, as Nature is (red of tooth and claw).

If tender folk go to pieces for fear a plant may be hurt (even before it is hurt, and it usually isn't), then how do they cope with the death of a dog or a person? We are not born to a guarantee of a voluptuous bonbon-type life, you know.

Give Me Strength — It's Spring

❀ YOU SHOULD NEVER START new gardening projects in the spring, although I do every year. Winter, you will notice, is a great incubation period for plans, and when spring comes you commonly get going on the arbor, the pool, the summerhouse, the terrace paving, the brick walk, the retaining wall, the post and trellis over the kitchen door, the new tool shed, and the Lord only knows what else.

My assistant here (at home) asks if there is any compelling reason I cannot assist with the spring cleanup, apart from the fact that I am working on the new pool, the new posts, the lotus and papyrus paintings on the posts of the summerhouse, and so on. So it commonly happens that just as the daffodils are in full sway, the effect is somewhat diminished by bags of mortar, odd tiles, varnish, lumber, and so forth.

Every two years the lily pool must be drained and cleaned, and fall is the time to do it, after the tree leaves have all fallen. It is chilly then, but that is the easiest time anyway. Circumstances prevented my doing it at the time I told you to, so I have a rather unlovely sight: the hundred-square-foot pool is drained of its water now, with about six inches of black ooze on the bottom.

This must all be shoveled out and put somewhere. Then the floor of the pool must be scrubbed. And before any of this happens, of course, the seven tubs of water lilies (all started into new growth) and vast quantities of seaweed must be boarded temporarily in great standby tanks of water — they cannot be left out in the air even for several hours, let alone the several days it takes me to clean the pool.

A thing the books never make clear is the ill temper that may be unavoidable in moving tubs of water lilies.

A plastic container holding thirty to forty quarts of wet earth is not a pleasant playmate in any body-contact sport (and I have nine altogether, not counting the tropicals, which are sulking in indoor aquarium durance), but it must be closely encountered, indeed, grappled with.

There is no way one man can lift one of these creatures out of the water. Not only are they immensely heavy, but the sides of the tubs are slimy. All three dogs commonly assist, yet fail to speed up the operation. Members of the household, far less eager than the dogs when invited to "give a hand here" do not enjoy helping move the tubs back once the pool is cleaned for another two years.

Nothing in the garden is really difficult. Everything can be managed by an ordinary imbecile; indeed, that is why it is the greatest of all amusements. The only thing is that every operation takes time.

"Stake the peonies," say the books, rightly, and any fool can stake a peony. Only not at the same moment he is varnishing an arch, weeding out violets, tying back Madame (both 'Madame Alfred Carrière' and 'Madame Grégoire Staechelin' are among the most generous of climbing roses, and among the most glamorous, and among the most insistent at flinging themselves about), coddling the Japanese irises, scratching the new wisteria, digging post holes, planting peach trees, and so on and on.

I realize now, thanks to my assistant's pointing it out, that for some decades I regularly launch a major lumber-and-mortar project every spring, and this interferes with pruning, scratching, tying, and scrubbing operations.

In the future I shall undertake these projects in July, when the pace is less frantic. Now the thing is, you want to get all your weeds out by mid-September so that nothing over-winters (or not much), and you want your painting projects finished then.

Vigorous climbing roses, needless to say, should be trimmed back a bit if they have produced fifteen-foot shoots, and tied rather firmly in the fall. You also want to be sure the lily pool is cleaned out in the fall, since there will hardly be time to do it in the spring.

And now that I know when to do things, I shall of course never have any trouble in the future.

Thomas Jefferson, an Optimistic Gardener

THOMAS JEFFERSON, that extraordinary gardener, reckoned among his benefactions the introduction of the olive tree to South Carolina, and never mind if till this day the Carolinians cannot grow olives.

In the same way, he wrote in 1781 that among the edible crops of Virginia were pomegranates, and while it was probably true that there was an eccentric gardener or two within the commonwealth who finally managed to get a pomegranate fruit from a bush grown against a south wall, the inclusion of pomegranates among the agricultural riches of the dominion was misleading at best and asinine at worst.

But any gardener will always understand Jefferson's olives (and other gardening enthusiasms) perfectly. Jefferson's astonishing garden at Monticello, overlooking the university town of Charlottesville, existed not only in red-clay reality but, even better, in Jefferson's imagination.

The first plantings at Monticello were made in 1770, but it was only in 1807 that the garden as we see it today got under way. As you leave the house from the salon you enter the big west lawn with its roundabout walk, a wide pathway that curves about in sinuous waves, not for any good practical or aesthetic reason but simply because straight paths would have meant a shorter walk, and Jefferson was fond of walking about. Besides, all the fine old gardens of Virginia since the early 1600s had had straight garden paths, and Jefferson loved newfangled ideas, in gardening as in everything else.

He laid out large oval beds for flowers in the angles of the house, which might strike one as curious since he said the house was embowered with sycamores, and not even Jefferson can count on luxuriant flowers beneath sycamores.

In fact, of Jefferson's trees at the house only two remain, and these are the yellow poplar, a tree rarely recommended for planting near a dwelling as it is forever dropping flowers or leaves or branches. Copper beeches were great favorites, too, and one survived until recently. The beeches make a dense shade, beneath which nothing will grow except snowdrops if you are lucky.

But all these sniveling modern objections would have meant nothing to Jefferson. He asked himself what are the most beautiful of all trees, and if he came up with sycamores, beeches, yellow poplars, and black locusts, who can argue with him? They may have defects as a practical matter, which is why current "tree experts" never recommend them near a house, but Jefferson thought beauty was worth a little inconvenience.

Often, or indeed always, when Jefferson was away, he worked on the Monticello garden in his head. It was clear that his gardening projects were entirely too optimistic (silkworms, maple syrup, wine comparable to that of France) but his solution to problems of skilled and plentiful garden labor, a chancy water supply, and his own absence from the garden was simple. Just make more elaborate plans than before.

This broadening of scope is the single most definitive quality of the true gardener: if you fail in small things and cannot perfectly manage your small garden, then expand and take on three times as much. That is gardening orthodoxy and Jefferson believed it with all his heart.

Peter J. Hatch, director of gardens and grounds at Monticello, has written that Jefferson was "crazy about gardening," and the adjective is well chosen. The mere fact that chinaberry trees do not survive on the stormy plateau of the garden did not stop Jefferson from planting them. The mere fact that transporting and planting copper beeches is full of risk even today did not prevent Jefferson's determination to have them shipped by wagon or by God to his garden from Washington, and if they perished then he tried again and if necessary yet again. He was going to have them and he did. Normal folk would give up at the first disaster.

Jefferson loved the native flowers, like the scarlet lobelias of the river bottoms amid the Virginia bluebells of the woods. He never got over the Carolina sweet shrub or the Carolina jasmine, and fully a fourth of the species of plants he grew were native Americans.

But Jefferson was never one of those squinty-eyed puritanical people who fear all propriety is violated if a tree from China and a fig from France share space with tulips from Turkey, irises from Yugoslavia, and dogwoods from Albemarle County.

His taste was catholic. He rather hoped the Lewis and Clark expedition to the Far West would find a nice mammoth for the Monticello park (they truly are extinct, but you never know till you really search) and new plants for Monticello — and of course for the betterment of gardens throughout the republic. Flowering currants were among the trophies.

Apart from the flowers of the garden, there was a two-acre vegetable garden, marvelously sunny, in the lee of a thousand-foot-long stone wall. This was sometimes full of weeds (a well-documented fact, but any gardener with two acres of vegetables would know that by instinct), but it also was full of beans, grown on arbors for their pretty flowers in purple and red.

And Jefferson must have loved broccoli, as he grew whole rows of green, purple, and white variations. How shocked the great man would be to learn that not all leaders of the republic share his wholesome taste. He grew twenty kinds of cabbage and roughly a million varieties of green peas, his favorite vegetable.

Like all gardeners, he was forever swapping plants and seeds. When he was in Paris he had things grown in Virginia shipped to France, and he planted perhaps the first golden-rain tree in America from a seed (only one grew) sent from France. He grew a cucumber from Ohio two feet long. Don't ask why. He just did.

Jefferson had eight acres devoted to a fruit garden, where he grew over the years more than a thousand fruit trees, including thirty-eight varieties of peaches and fourteen cherries. He grew apricots and almonds for the precious refreshment (as he put it) of their fruit. The fact that he grew apricots and almonds for a particular refreshment does not mean, necessarily, that he got anything edible from them.

He also grew twenty-four kinds of European wine grapes. These did not succeed in any great way. Virginians had scarcely settled in at Jamestown before they tried wine grapes, but whether anything actually drinkable was ever produced at Monticello in Jefferson's day depends on what one considers drinkable. Jefferson drank Château d'Yquem and Château Margaux and Muscat de Frontignan. He had little taste for the nasty.

He imported the 'White Marseilles' fig, which he considered supreme and which today is still considered about as good as figs get. A high wood paling fence three-quarters of a mile long enclosed the fruit and vegetable gardens. The boards were ten feet high and so closely spaced the poor wild rabbits could not get in. Or so Jefferson said.

There cannot have been an inch of the 5,000-acre farm, from the summit 867 feet above sea level to the damp fringes of the Rivanna flowing at its base, that Jefferson did not know intimately. He often worked in the garden himself, sometimes half an hour at a time in the cool of the evening. That much is documented.

For the rest, he was obliged to fuss, in a caring way, of course, at his daughters and granddaughters, who for some reason did not work all day every day to keep weeds at bay and who did not (for the young rarely have steady habits) keep meticulous records such as the date of the first lilacs, the last fall of the beech leaves. It is probably true that these women — good women, splendid women, but not fully attentive — did not even know how many beans are needed to fill a pint jar.

Jefferson did.

There are many pretty gardens in America, but few gardens outlast their owner, and Jefferson's fell to ruin after his death in 1826. Its restoration began in 1939, and only now are the vegetable and fruit gardens coming into shape. But then these things take time. One of Jefferson's most endearing qualities was his serenity in the face of garden disasters, which were as frequent at Monticello as anywhere

else. You win some, lose some. That was Jefferson's garden philosophy. You keep on planting stuff. If it failed last year, try giving it more
rotted manure this year. And look here, my dear, here's a fellow out
West who grew a six-pound tomato — well, we must write immediately and get seeds.

Gardening Pains and Pleasures

NO PAIN, NO GAIN, and that is why my garden has gained so
little over the years, I guess. To me a garden is no place for pain.
You can find enough of that at the office.

Of course, nature herself provides plenty of pain for the gardener,
but we learn to take her lumps, and as long as we don't race about
making a lot of extra pain for ourselves (trimming verges, spraying
chemicals about, and such) the garden is fairly joyful.

At the moment I have a number of slight wounds inflicted on both
arms by a dasylirion, a plant I dearly love and had vast trouble
finding. It is native to Texas and northern Mexico, so it is not likely to
be hardy, but no great harm comes from trying, and I promise not to
groan and mope about if it dies next winter. The dasylirions are
related to agaves, the century plants, and resemble yuccas, except that
instead of shooting off at sharp angles, the dasylirion leaves (which
are only half an inch wide, with little spines along both edges) arc
out. They make a pretty fountain of green. When they eventually
bloom, the stalk is fifteen feet high, but for practical purposes they
make a fine mound of elegant green, like a very slender weeping
yucca.

In its own country the plant is called sotol, which I think is the
name of some booze made from it; even more commonly it is called
bear grass. A number of plants are called bear grass, especially the
hesperaloes, which look like thin yuccas with red flowers. The botanical name means thick lily, probably in allusion to the dense tuft
of leaves and its vague relationship to true lilies.

Anyhow, while I was planting the dasylirion last week, the spines got me and made a lot of little red dots. I went to a doctor about something else and when they took my blood pressure I suspect my arms looked as if I had been making a lot of hypodermic injections. I looked as spacy as possible for the technician, hoping she would say something to the doctor, "Did you SEE his arms?"

One thing I am sure of, it is rarely a good idea to explain anything.

Living to Grow Another Day

❈ ONE OF THE WONDERS of early spring is the star magnolia, and let's begin by forbidding every gardener from the usual whines, snarls, and curses that the flowers of this elegant little tree are frozen in two springs out of four. So they are. Nothing to be done about it. The only question is whether the star magnolia is worth growing, and the answer is an absolute unqualified yes.

I used to have one that had deep pink flowers instead of the usual white. Its buds were red, but it opened pink. That form is called *Magnolia stellata rubra.* There are other variants, some with garden-variety names, and all of them are good.

The blooms are three inches wide, composed of a dozen or more strappy petals of suede texture. The stamens in the center are not conspicuous, but the perfume of the flowers is glorious and spicy, suggesting clove and lily of the valley.

The scent of the great southern evergreen magnolia, *M. grandiflora,* is almost rank by comparison. Most of the fragrant magnolias have a lemony scent, strong and agreeable to most noses, but the scent of the star magnolia is the only one I can think of that is supremely sweet.

Now is a good time to plant all magnolias, giving them quite a bit of peat moss or humus in their planting site and attention to watering their first summer if there should be a dry spell.

It may as well be faced that early spring is a time of occasional frosts. When spring comes in March, as it does, and when the last freeze of thirty-two degrees comes in mid-April, as it does at my place, a freeze or two can be expected. We can even have a freeze in May.

Thomas Jefferson had a murderous freeze well into May one year at Monticello, and nothing became the man better than his equanimity at the disaster. As he said, the failures of one thing are offset by the success of other things. Very likely the okra was good the same year that half the plants of Monticello were killed.

One year within living memory the olive trees of the Rhone Valley were killed outright — even old trees. Nature is not run like a good clock but like a good (more or less) dog. Snarls sometimes. There should be a book, *When a Good Spring Does Bad Things.*

Our expectations are based, if we are reasonable, and many gardeners are not, on general experience. Usually January is cold and June is warm, but not always. Usually peach trees set fruit, but not always. Usually tomatoes ripen in July, but not always.

Much annoyance and fretful muttering could be avoided if we got it into our heads at the beginning of our gardening (it usually takes about twenty years) that nothing is guaranteed. But average experience over the centuries shows that gardening is the best of all bets in a chancy world.

Sometimes I hear alarmed cries from youngish gardeners that their neighbors' daffodils or tulips or whatnot are in full bloom while those planted carefully by our gardener in October are not. It is not always realized that in their first spring newly planted bulbs come into flower about ten days later than those of established clumps. Take a popular daffodil like 'February Gold'. It may bloom anytime from late February to early April in Washington, depending on the vagaries of the season. With me it usually flowers on March 15 or 16. But whenever it flowers, new bulbs (that is, those planted the fall before) bloom ten days later. Once they have settled in, the blooms of this daffodil and all others may be expected to bloom at the same time; thus 'February Gold' will bloom March 16 whether planted two falls or ten falls ago.

Good deeds in the garden are often punished, so I am not too surprised to see that my young ten-foot plant of the 'White Marseilles' fig is bent at a 45-degree angle. That is because I set a rather large Christmas tree against its south side in January to protect it from wind, cold, and too sudden warming by the south sun of early March, which might inspire it to sprout out then, only to be frozen back.

Unfortunately, the hurricane winds of the March blizzard hit the protective Christmas tree with such force that the fig was much bent. I shall do nothing, as within two or three years the fig will straighten itself up (by new shoots) and you will never know how bent it was in the spring of 1993.

This may be the place to say that fig trees are sometimes killed back in Washington and sometimes killed all the way to the ground, after which they require two years to start fruiting again. If I had my choice, I'd plant figs against a wall facing west. Instead, for reasons of convenience, I have two figs facing east and one facing south. I may as well expect that every four or five years they will be damaged.

We shall have some nippy days, even following some days of almost hot weather. But now is the time to plant all shrubs that were not planted in the fall. A good time for hollies, photinias, magnolias, redbuds, azaleas, vitex, kerrias, and roses (assuming you have been too lazy to plant them between November and the end of February), but do not doze by the fire waiting for balmy days. When they come they will come with a fury, bringing greater stress to the plants than would be the case if they had been planted earlier.

Budding Romance

FOR A LONG TIME when I was a kid, my malaria would come back at just this time of year, and first you burn up, then you freeze, and it goes on for some days. Like any sick puppy I hated it, but now I think the misery was not all bad, but maybe strengthened the blood against some worse sickness, who knows. Besides, sometimes I got flowers and had hours to look at them.

In any case I am never surprised to go off my feed for a couple of days at this time of year, knowing all will be right as rain.

But I mention it because I've seen in other gardeners a tendency to gaze at some flower as if glued to the spot and unaware of anything else. At first the gardener has the queasy feeling he's falling in love with a flower. But as years pass he sees that some common flower has turned magical on him, to such an extent that a bizarre bonding has occurred. Normal people, he suspects, do not enter a lifelong union with a flower.

As I say, that is what the young gardener thinks. Later on he accepts it. Thereafter he is half himself and half willow or viburnum or whatever object it is that has taken possession of him. It can be anything, but it is always a flower he thinks is uniquely beautiful and significant, and usually there are only a few that seduce him with such force.

It is unwise to brush off the action of a flower, since it can be a thing close to the soul and not merely some whim, as one might prefer one mustard to another. It is more like an enlightenment that can have effect well past a garden wall. The thing is not to be frightened of it.

Just the other day I sneaked out to see if that white flower out there was not the pretty old trumpet daffodil 'Cantatrice'. As if I wouldn't know it out my window a mile off. And what a pleasure to see it once again, and what a great glow of having put one over on Fate, because although this flower has grown like a weed in this scrawny cat-run of a garden for so long now, there were whole decades in which I could not grow it at all. Couldn't keep it even for two years in my former garden a thousand miles from here.

When I discovered I could grow it here — I like to say any jobber-nowl can — I was as pleased as a dog with two tails. Or a pilgrim in sight of Jerusalem.

Before being dragged back to the house somewhat wheezy, I silently differed from one other person who went on about "death of cold" and "even turkeys sometimes have sense to come in from the rain." A cantatrice is a beautiful singer, the kind, I suppose, that sits on rocks and lures sailors to their doom, or maybe something not so grim. Any gardener, once he gets set in his ways, will find a few flowers that work like talismans or magical beasts. I have even known gardeners who choked up at clover fields or geese chomping Johnson grass in the cotton. They don't say so, but when they see the field or the flower they know they are on holy ground.

There is nothing wrong with that gardener's head. Except no mortal is strong enough to absorb what you may call 100-proof infusions from the farthest galaxies, not strong enough to bear the surge from the farthest core of life. He may pretend he has not known it, but it does him no good. He has known. Right there in front of him was the blessed cantatrice and he was not the same as he formerly was.

At first we laugh it out, we talk it out, we drink it out, lest we should be converted and the flower should heal us.

The gardener knows the mud will slop the bloom. Or even if it doesn't, the white daffodils will last no more than a week or two or at most four. But it is bad for his life to forget what passed between the cantatrice and him. The world does not have to know, and even the gardener might require years before he at last knows his life with the flower is not unwise.

In school there was a man of honor and polish who did his unwearying best to teach us blank-eyed bumpkins a little Greek. He coughed every year when he got to that part of Socrates' speech in which the mother of Achilles (and she was a goddess) speaks to him before his death. Even as boys we knew *The Iliad* at that point was not just a soldier's anecdote.

Another thing that was more than met the eye at first was that sketch of a Greek party long after the age of heroes where a roaring drunk crashed in — the golden Alcibiades, divinely smashed and unable to join the rest in their arguments about the nature of love. The wine scoured his poor brain, leaving only a direct perception of godly beauty in the person of that difficult and irritating philosopher Socrates. The drunk, famous for his beauty, saw himself as ugly when confronted by a philosopher whose body was no handsomer than a toad.

Sometimes he had to shut his ears when Socrates was talking, he blurted out. Otherwise the beauty of the old teacher would so seize his soul that he would grow old just sitting at his feet. The great thing here was that even a golden boy (not much admired by boys in school) when properly medicated could see a divine beauty far greater than his own, and could see the proper response to it. Divine beauty is where you find it probably. There is authority for the notion that God once spoke through a jackass, a real one with furry ears. But another time perhaps through a toad-faced philosopher? And beyond doubt, sometimes through a weather-defiant flower.

As if some dumb clod slogging through the dark should look up and see a dozen suns all blazing in the firmament. A good steady gardener, suspicious of blather and embarrassed by his own growing reverence for some stupid flower, will ask how to know if there is anything real going on, or if it's some pretty fantasy, some rather dangerous fantasy of the kind often taught to tots without regard to truth.

And you can't answer it for him. He will know sooner or later, and then it will make no difference what anybody says or thinks.

All this, then, to comfort the nervous gardener struck dumb by a flower. It is not terminal madness. It is the opening pitch (in many cases) of truth that is tricky even to attempt in words.

You do, even in paradise, have to come in from the rain, and of course from high glory as well, and scrub the dog's food bowl and get back to the office. Lofty is not everything. It's not even anything if it's just pretend.

All I know is it costs me little, and I think does me good, to keep always in center field, so to speak, the action of the cantatrice.

What happened with the flower is that the road gets wider, to such an expansion that the gardener is led far past a mere flower, however beautiful, to the outer courtyard, almost, of divine things.

What the right flower can do, with luck, is heal the gardener, making him fit (more or less) to love, by steps however slow. Growing old, still in awe, still sitting at her feet.

Not Everyone Wants to
Go Whole Hog into Gardening

❦ THE FRAGRANT VIBURNUMS of spring have been blooming, and I cannot think of a more worthwhile pair of shrubs than *V. juddii* and *V. plicatum* 'Mariesii'. The first has clusters of pink (fading to white) tubular flowers gathered together in a ball, and while I cannot describe the scent, it is slightly tinged with clove and is of the same quality as lily of the valley.

Its growth is densely twiggy, and while it is compact in shape it is no shrinking violet. I see mine has spread a few feet to one side, forcing a ten-foot holly to lean so far over the sidewalk that it will have to be severely sawed back.

The other viburnum is quite different and is scentless, but its horizontal branches are solid with flat clusters of white flowers. It blooms with the dogwoods or a few days later and is as showy as that tree. This viburnum bears fruit, but it usually drops off in early summer and thus does not count for anything, and the fall coloring of the leaves is pleasant but not gaudy, a soft buffy-orange-salmon. It grows to perhaps nine feet high and ten or twelve feet wide. If you want the same sort of viburnum only in a larger plant, the variety 'Lanarth' is ideal.

Often people do not want to go whole hog into gardening, and merely want things to look all right. For them the answer is a reasonable assortment of shrubs such as these and other viburnums.

And however common the flowering quinces may be, they are still first-rate shrubs. They come in pink, white, orange, and scarlet, and in time form globular plants six or seven feet high, but are easily pruned to lower heights if you prefer. The large occasional fruits can be made into preserves. I did that once but never ate the stuff; possibly you could send them for Christmas presents.

A few evergreens would keep the shrub grouping cheerful in winter. In shady spots in Zone 7, nothing is prettier than skimmias, which bloom in a modest way in April, but the glory of the plant is the scarlet fruit, like small cherries, in abundance all winter. This plant goes well with camellias.

Dwarf yews add black-green to the palette, but be sure they are dwarf, as both Japanese and English yews soon grow to second-story heights and beyond.

In Washington the climate is so favorable that many an evergreen azalea can be grown in a mixed border of shrubs, requiring no particular attention but appreciative of a permanent mulch of oak leaves.

At the fringes of the various shrubs, where they meet a lawn, say, there can be plantings of daffodils. A good effect is had by planting a dozen of one variety in an oval or fish shape three feet long. Of course, if twenty-five or a hundred bulbs are thus used, the effect is more striking, but even a dozen bulbs are handsome.

Such a scheme would not satisfy a deep-dyed gardener but would bring much pleasure with virtually no labor to the new homeowner who is perhaps much preoccupied with small tots and a terrier and a job.

A slightly more ambitious scheme would involve a boundary planting of the shrubs and perhaps a small tree such as a dogwood, then a sunny spot for flowers. A grand combination consists of daffodils (for March and April flowers) followed by irises (for May) and daylilies (for late June to August).

Once I saw a plan for using these three splendid perennials together, and followed it with unhappy results. It involved a checkerboard design, each square two feet. Square 1 would be daffodils, Square 2 would be irises, Square 3 would be daylilies. The trouble was that the irises promptly overstepped the bounds of their square, and the daylilies produced longer leaves than expected and started to swamp the irises, which then wanted to take over the daffodils.

No. A better plan is to put a clump of daylilies and a clump of irises in front of each clump of daffodils. Plant them three feet in front of the daffodils and three feet apart. If you think you have too many daffodils, simply substitute a daylily or iris clump in place of them here and there. The point is that both irises and daylilies grow up to conceal the dying daffodil leaves in May and June, and you have fine flowers for four months or more.

The trick is to allow three feet between your iris and daylily clumps, or even four feet if they are very large clumps. The temptation is to plant them a foot apart, and that means endless sweat and heave-ho by the end of the first year.

You can plant the new irises and so on a foot apart and then take out every other one (to plant elsewhere) the second year, and after another two years again remove every other clump. That way you wind up with your large clumps well spaced, but in the meantime you do not have the weeding of large beds with widely spaced plants.

It is a help to mulch the beds with two inches or more of wood chips or something of the kind, or you can use one of those "landscape fabrics," taking care to get the kind that lets water through but keeps weeds from growing up.

This is Scarlet O'Hara time in the garden. Tomorrow is another day.

May

The Perfect Moment

WE ARE NOW at high spring, with a few days of glorious sun and temperatures in the seventies. So many things to do and left undone. My scientific cords to keep the tree peonies from falling into the fish pool have collapsed. I thought they would.

And for the third year, what am I to do with 'Susan Treadwell'? This is a lemony daylily I bought years ago from Scheepers. It blooms late, that is in mid-July or after, and its formerly ideal position between two horse troughs is no longer ideal. The mutt has discovered the narrow passage and Susan is at risk.

The old alba rose 'Celeste' needs tying to her post again, as does the rambler 'Ginny'. How they get loose from the telephone cables used to secure them to their poles I have no idea.

Ivy has gotten into two favorite peonies, 'Red Charm' and 'M. Jules Elie', so they are not going to bloom well. On the other hand, two peonies are about to bloom that I only vaguely recall having planted as wee snippets several years ago.

So many things in a garden are purely optional. A matter of preference. But two bulbs I consider indispensable in every garden, no matter the size, are the sky-blue *Ipheion uniflorum,* with blue stars on eight-inch stems and with fountains or tussocks of glaucous, thin, strappy leaves that smell like garlic. The flowers, however, smell like violets. They bloom with daffodils and camellias and well into the azalea season. They are permanent and form clumps. As they are not expensive, every gardener should start off with fifty or so.

Equally reliable are the Spanish squills, long known as *Scilla campanulata*, now called *Endymion hispanicus*. The best ones are blue, and the best blue is 'Excelsior', which I used to grow. Its bells are borne on stems almost two feet high. The others, in various pretty tints of rose, lavender, and white, are about a foot in height. They are one of the few bulbs that persist for decades, perhaps centuries. They are planted in the fall, and they bloom with the utmost regularity just before (and with) the tall bearded irises.

I began to see flower stalks emerging on the irises on April 25. They should be in bloom about May 7 to May 10, each clump in beauty for two weeks.

I miss my annual azalea argument with Joseph Alsop, now with God but for a long time a political columnist who managed at one time or another to delight, inform, and infuriate everybody in the capital.

He loved to taunt me on the matter of magenta azaleas, which I admire. He felt the best people had only white azaleas, and I enjoyed taunting him that his favorite, 'Snow', was rather a poor azalea, as it holds its old blossoms when they turn brown. This enraged him, in a gentlemanly sort of way. The best white, by the way, is the Glenn Dale 'Treasure'.

Judd's viburnum (*V. juddii*) is in perfection, perfuming the sidewalk for some distance. It blooms all at once and is in beauty for perhaps no more than a week. That is true of so many flowers in our favorable climate, which has blue skies and sun. In bleak places such as England it probably blooms for a month.

Tree peonies have flowers roughly the size of soup plates, and for some weeks their flower buds, at first no larger than a pea, grow to golf-ball size. Then without warning these opulent gorgeous flowers spring forth like clowns from a Volkswagen. How does so much floral tissue get crammed into those buds? The same is true of many poppies, of course.

The pools did not get their mid-December cleanup. That is because I was too lazy and too cold to do it. No excuse. I am thinking of convincing myself that I left the pools alone for the sake of the dragonfly nymphs down in the mulm.

With tender new leaves and flowers all about, it is easy for the gardener to think he has done well. Payday will come in summer, when all defects shall be revealed. This is Scarlett O'Hara time in the garden. Tomorrow is another day. These are the few days the gods give us to jump up and down in. Tomorrow, when all that is wrong will be evident in the garden — tomorrow, well I say tomorrow is spinach and I say the hell with it.

The Cicadas, Bringing Their Sweet Symphony

EVERY GARDENER should rejoice that about May 14, favored parts of the capital will welcome once again the billions of melodious cicadas. These elegant insects, sometimes called locusts, come every spring and summer, but only after seventeen endless years below ground. It takes that long for the egg to develop into the rainbow-winged adult.

They emerge through small holes in the earth and crawl up stems or trunks to split their old constricting garments and (allowing a few minutes for hardening the iridescent wings) soar through the incense-laden airs of a Washington May.

Their song, which is glorious, is made by vibrating their wings, using the cavity of the thorax as a sounding chamber, very like a cello. We shall have cicadas for about six weeks, but it seems to me the most melodious chorus lasts only a fortnight.

A full half-century ago, when I was in Paris, I was told of the beautiful song of the *cigale* in the valley of the Rhone, so I went there to hear it. I thought it was a kind of nightingale. Imagine my surprise — every olive tree was full of cicadas, and while I was glad I went, I could not help noticing that their cicadas are not so beautiful as ours, nor is their music as sweet.

Although we have cicadas every year, and all of them have endured long years below ground, it is only once every seventeen years that we have Brood 10 (the greatest brood of all), so that instead of one cicada on the screen door (as in ordinary years) we have dozens resting on every fire hydrant, three on every rose leaf. They eat nothing in their few short weeks in the sun. It is unthinkable to kill them with sprays — they do no harm. As for chemical poisons in the garden, you probably remember when DDT was spread about with abandon in virtually every garden in America, though its sale at garden centers has now been forbidden by the same government that once smiled on its use.

The only thing the cicada does is make little slits in twigs to lay its eggs, which duly drop to the earth to begin the long years of development underground. A few twigs here and there have never done any harm in my garden, though we have cicadas by the thousand in a great year such as this one [1987].

Some people do not like the vibrating noise of the locust. They are the same people who do not mind jackhammers, trucks, gasoline mowers, chain saws, and all the other inventions of the Devil that make gardening outdoors less of a pleasure than it used to be. The cicadas, at least, were designed by God. All right-thinking gardeners consider them one of the great ornaments of the garden.

Fortunately they are not endangered, they are not near extinction, but every gardener has a responsibility not to harm them.

The Maryland Cooperative Extension Service advises against spraying cicadas. If you are one of those nervous-Nellie people, you can cover your trees with some kind of netting or cheesecloth, the extension service says, with little regard for the absurdity of trying to do that.

As for the sound the cicadas make, you can kill the innocent creatures by the million and still not stop the sound, short of gassing the entire capital. Which some imbecile will probably suggest in due time, having no comprehension of the opposition he will meet.

I should add that cicadas do not sting, bite, or otherwise harm humans, even when picked up. As F. Eugene Wood, an extension entomologist at the University of Maryland so rightly says, "They don't hurt anyone and they're not a health threat, so we might as well enjoy them while we can."

He recommends bringing some of the newly emerged nymphs into school classrooms so students can watch them split their skins and emerge in their beautiful final form.

It is said that the Pilgrims misnamed them "locusts" in 1630, which is not surprising, if true, as they were frequently wrong about any number of things.

There are other cicadas that operate on a thirteen-year schedule, and they too have various broods that emerge in different years. In rare years a great thirteen-year brood emerges at the same time as our great Brood 10 of seventeen-year cicadas, and then they are everywhere. This last happened in the glorious year of 1970 and will not happen again for more than a century, the extension service informs me — too long to wait.

This year, in other words, we shall not have as many as we did in 1970, but we must make do with what we have.

Poisoning cicadas, the extension service points out, has many undesirable side effects, even beyond the outrageous slaughter of these handsome creatures. To kill cicadas you also have to kill many honeybees, and you help build up red spider mites (which do a great deal of damage in gardens) and other insect pests, since you kill beneficial insects that otherwise prey on them. Carbaryl (which kills cicadas, all right) also causes excessive fruit thinning on apple trees.

Our Indians used to eat cicadas, and so do many birds and squirrels, and pets often eat a few or even a great many. My hound Bass ate several thousand in 1970, a figure we arrived at by counting the number she ate on her two daily walks and multiplying by the number of days she walked during the cicada season.

Stopping to Smell the Rugosas

I SEE WE HAVE NOT paid enough attention to the rugosa roses. As all gardeners know, we lean toward things we cannot grow with safety, such as oleanders, gardenias, and the general flora of subtropical climes, and we take for granted the magnolias, nandinas, photinias, and so forth that we can grow and grow well.

And when it comes to things they can grow even in Boston and similar arctic places, well of course we will have none of that. We want the plants of the Gulf Coast or the Mediterranean, and we virtually sneer at anything that can be grown in colder climates than our own.

Thus, among roses, we may stir ourselves, at least in our thoughts, for the great tea roses that grow so well in Italy or Charleston, and many a gardener will go to a bit of trouble on behalf of somewhat tender kinds (they die if just plopped in anywhere, but may grow all right if given a warm wall and a bit of mulch and extra shelter in winter) like the Lady Banks Yellow or 'Maréchal Niel', the spectacularly scented butter-yellow noisette rose.

We may even condescend to grow some of the wild roses of Asia, hardy as oaks, provided they are uncommon (as they all are in American gardens), for we like to be the only fellow around with this or that treasure from Tibet.

But the rugosa rose and its varieties are somewhat scorned and always have been. The unspeakable beauty of the wild white rugosa made scarcely a dent on any gardening consciousness when it was introduced from Japan in the last century. Nobody then liked five-petaled wild roses, especially wild roses not even mentioned by Shakespeare.

And when it became clear that these rugosas were excellent for binding dunes along the Massachusetts coast, they were even less esteemed than ever. How could a rose be worth growing if Yankees can grow it in a wilderness?

All the same, the rugosas are among the most glorious of roses, often highly perfumed, virtually foolproof, and usually of splendid habit in the garden, unlike the floribundas and hybrid teas, which do not make handsome bushes at all.

By the end of April I saw that my yellow rugosa, 'Agnes', was in flower. This is a hybrid of the wild rugosa and the wild yellow rose of Persia, *R. foetida*. 'Agnes' is buff, a soft color, a butter-buff with a hint of brown about it. The flowers are double, showing the stamens when wide open, and like all rugosas it is no good for cutting unless you are content with four-inch stems. The leaves are deeper than medium green and have a leathery quality.

The scent is attar of roses with an undertone not entirely pure, as if a pinch of asafetida were back there somewhere. Furthermore, the scent does not waft abroad on the air; you have to get right up on the bloom to smell it.

Another good one is 'Belle Poitevine', which in bud is rich cherry, but which opens to medium madder with a touch of magenta. Later in the season it has fruit like cherries. 'Agnes' does not.

One of the grand ones is 'Roseraie de l'Haÿ', named for the rose garden out from Paris. It is deep rose-red, a muted rich magenta sometimes, or rose approaching purple. It has as fine a scent as any rose in cultivation and would be worth growing for that alone, but also it makes a fine bush maybe five feet high and wide. Unfortunately, it does not seem to be in general commerce, but I have noticed that if gardeners fuss and mutter long enough, unobtainable plants have a way of eventually showing up in catalogues.

This rose I had to order from England, a substantial pain, and it had to be isolated for two years out in the country before I was able to plant it in my garden. You have to want a plant badly to go through the process.

'Hansa' is a red-purple rugosa, strong of clove scent and ferociously armed, but then most rugosas — all I have ever dealt with — have thorns to make a porcupine blush. They are sheer hell to prune, and I find I do not prune them unless they get so large they threaten to take over the place. A good saw in winter is the best tool for them.

'Sarah Van Fleet' was once a popular pink rugosa (a slightly raw candy-pink), heavily perfumed and invariably making a good solid bush. Mine is about eight feet high. Then this rose fell into disfavor, and now (for such is the fickle nature of gardeners) it is becoming esteemed once more. It blooms off and on all season as most of the rugosas do, except 'Agnes'.

If you want a white sort, 'Blanc Double de Coubert' is all right — I am not as smitten with it as most rugosa enthusiasts seem to be — and 'Sir Thomas Lipton' is a possibility. It looks quite ratty (or its blooms do) all summer and fall, but at the end of April it covers itself with white roses the quality of white camellias, only scented. Besides these, the single white rugosa listed as 'Rugosa Alba' seems to me flawless.

I have never sprayed any rugosa, and while they are not immune to black spot, they do not go into a blue funk over it. All the rugosas turn a nice russet-yellow in the fall, nothing spectacular, but pleasant enough since most roses have foliage that does not color at all.

The Gardener's Life Is Full of Woe

❀ ALMOST EVERY SPRING is normal, but no spring pleases the gardener altogether. A few hot days, and cries go up that flowers are stewed; a few gray days in the fifties, and the gardener predicts a new Ice Age.

I have a new weed with a root like a parsnip. The trick is to wait for good rains or to water heavily, then grasp the stems in a bunch and pull straight up. Pull to the side and the root remains. Delay and the roots break off to bring trouble another year. Let the weed go to seed and there will be years of pulling.

Weeds are clever and produce vast numbers of seeds, which sprout when conditions are right, but not all the first year or even the fifth year. They wait in the ground almost forever, so the trick is to prevent seeding in the first place.

Among flowers bedded out for summer bloom, one of the best is the snapdragon. I had a friend who bought young plants eight inches high at a grocery store every year and made four-inch cuttings when he got them home, thus tripling the number of plants. If done in early May it works, especially with the dwarf snapdragons popular today.

Names of tree peonies are often confused when plants are not bought from specialists, but I have half a dozen bought at a hardware store and have no complaint. The colors are white, light pink, red, red-purple, and what I guess is coral of remarkable brilliance and light. The first ones opened April 25, while others still have fat buds in early May. Like many of the most beautiful flowers, they last in perfection no more than a week, and usually four days.

We have some new hostas along a hundred-foot walk with five arches of roses along its way, though it ends rather ingloriously with a solid wood gate beyond which are the alley and the garbage cans.

Hostas do not show their surprising effectiveness until they make fat clumps, a matter of three years. None of them likes a sunny spot, so they are ideal plants for woodsy gardens (or small-town gardens surrounded by buildings or overhung by trees). I have a fondness for a degree of gaudiness, using hostas with blue leaves and with golden leaves together. If the ultimate effect is unsettling, nothing is easier (as garden things go) than digging them up and shifting them to other spots to avoid the contrasts. I have the great contrasts ('Blue Umbrellas' with 'Gold Standard', for instance) at the near end of the walk, toned down a little by a large upright yew tree. Farther along I have only green and blue-gray varieties. Eighty feet down the path I have 'Tall Boy', which has flower stems of shoulder height, because I am a pushover for any flower of conspicuous altitude.

Plants with big leaves also delight me. This year I have gathered several small plants of butterbur, *Petasites japonicus giganteus,* into a twenty-four-inch tub. This will prevent the roots' roaming about and coming up in unexpected and disastrous places. Often when a plant is utterly distinct from everything else, and especially if its goal is to attain high weedship and take over the county, it can be stashed in a tub of rich earth, somewhat like a genie in a bottle.

A beautiful but dangerous plant is the blue lyme grass, which is too invasive for civilized places, but if confined in a tub or concrete box its beauty can be enjoyed. Yet another candidate for tubdom, except that it does not like being confined, is the plume poppy.

There must be gardeners who grow successfully the somewhat tender giant gunnera from Chile. I once saw a picture of a man sitting on horseback beneath a vast leaf. I have never seen this plant with a leaf greater than six feet across, but they can grow larger. Unfortunately, I have never succeeded with it. The gardener's life is full of woe.

The British Deal with Downpours

AS YOU KNOW, it usually rains in the spring, and as I write we are seven inches wetter than normal for the date, so this year we can complain of the water as last year we could complain of its lack. As a help to readers somewhat sodden amid their irises and tomatoes, and to keep us all in an honest perspective, and also to offer a helpful hint, I now cite Dr. Lindley's solution to downpours.

Dr. Lindley was president of the Royal Horticultural Society in the 1840s in London. The society (as I learned in its most recent journal) had been blessed with many years of superb weather for its spring shows. Nobody even thought about bad weather for these grand events.

And then, I believe it was 1849 though memory dims, at a particularly grand fete the heavens opened up. Nobody would have come in the first place, except that they had paid a lot for their tickets and besides the patrons were quite grand, so everybody came hoping the rain would stop shortly.

It got worse shortly. The men gallantly slid all the food off the great silver salvers (setting the food on the table itself) and sat the ladies on the beautiful silver trays. Merriment ran high, as did occasional exasperated cross words. Dr. Lindley ordered more and more champagne to be brought, and this apparently did much to keep guests from snarling.

But then word came to Dr. Lindley that the tents and temporary wooden structures sheltering the guests were about to collapse, as their supporting poles were wobbling in the mud.

Dr. Lindley lost no time. "With his usual fertility of resource he instantly sent agents into the streets, pot-houses, barns, and smithies of Chiswick and Turnham Green wherever men in a rainy day most congregate.

"'Hire,' said he, 'every man you can get. Don't stand upon the price. Give them one shilling an hour, two shillings, five shillings, whatever they require, but hire them instantly and send them in at once.'

"As the men came, they were posted in clumps around every pillar and support to hold them up, while the unconscious guests reveled within. Matters became worse. It was only by main force that the buildings were sustained."

If you think a show must go on, that's nothing compared with a major event of the Royal Horticultural Society. So it went on. At last the guests began to leave in their carriages. But wait! The weather lightened in early evening.

"The guests paused in their departure and determined on a fresh effort at enjoyment. The musicians, who had retired to obtain their own refreshment, were recalled from the public-houses to which they had retreated in order to enable the guests to terminate the fete with dancing, and on the wet and splashy grass dancing was for some short time kept up."

It was not all that much fun, however, and at last the guests all left. The men who had been holding up the posts were dismissed, and the tents and buildings gave way, "burying in one undistinguishable ruin the tables, the dinner service, wines and viands under their wet and heavy folds."

Dr. Lindley said just let things be till Monday. It was, however, two weeks before all the silver plate, quite valuable, was recovered. The society's servants were a credit indeed. Not a single piece was lost. The spoons and forks were raked out of the mud, and not one (the society was pleased to report) was missing.

So you see. Next time your house and the rose arbors and so forth threaten to collapse in the rain, simply emulate Dr. Lindley. Hire stout fellows from the bars and barns and pay them a shilling or so to hold everything up till the world is dry again.

And now that we are in our best-of-all-possible-worlds mood, I cite further good news from England. The great garden of Leonardslee in Sussex was grievously hurt by the gale a couple of years ago, the collection of conifers almost destroyed and many superb trees of the main gardens lost.

But just as at Yellowstone, the disaster had its silver lining. The rhododendrons are now getting more light and blooming better than ever. And for almost a century now the park beyond the main garden has been home to wallabies, splendid fuzzy beasts like small kangaroos and of Australian origin. The climate at Leonardslee is so mild the animals have carried on through the years.

They were always excluded from the main garden, of course. But after the great storm the fences were so badly damaged that the wallabies flooded in to the most carefully tended parts of the garden. It has turned out they do no damage at all and moreover nibble the grass, an activity resulting in reduced labor for the men. They would eat young plants, but then so would rabbits, so tender young plants are already protected by wire netting.

The wallabies bounding about in the main garden have given pleasure to visiting kids and (if they but admitted it) adults. So to hell with the power of storms. Let the wallabies bloom.

After the Rain, a Deluge of Tasks

❀ BY TODAY we'll have seen the sun again in this sodden capital, and while the endless rains of May have sent gardeners into what may fairly be called a substantial snit, they have done no damage to plants. This month of deluge is better, after all, than a spring drought.

The past week I planted out several dahlias. They were in six-inch pots, stocky and vigorous, about a foot high, and they gave me a sense of triumph as I started them indoors and brought them to a kind of perfection without artificial light, just on a desk by a window.

It is surprising how much protection a porch gives. The wind is tempered though the cold is not. The young plants got more light than they did in the house. When knocked out of their pots the root balls were dense with roots but not yet too crowded.

A terrible problem for the gardener who has no labor but his own, however, is deciding whether the dahlias need to be planted out more than the fence requires repairing or the walkway needs weeding — deciding, in short, between the need for maintenance and the need for playing with plants.

If the element of play is not present, there is no point in gardening at all. And yet, to give an example, it was decided two months ago to move a circular horse trough (used for fish and water lilies) about a hundred feet to a better site. The water was drained, the ferocious mat of roots in six inches of mulm at the bottom of the pool was eventually removed, and the water lilies were cut apart, their tubs of mud emptied and removed, and all was ready for lifting and rolling the tank.

There has been no chance in that two months to get the job done. Now the empty tank has six inches of water in it from rainfall and must be drained anew. In the meantime plants along the route to the new site have grown fabulously and will be more damaged than if they were small and the job had been done as originally planned.

So that great task hangs over me, yet now the pokeweed and bindweed have started and must not be allowed to gain any foothold. The nearly wild clematis (white with purple edges) that was trained nicely into a crimson rose and onto an arch of a white rambler has taken advantage of the rains and sent long shoots away from the roses. If these are not promptly tucked back where they belong, it will be impossible later to get the desired effect of billowing white roses spotted with violet.

So many things in the spring must be done immediately if they are to be done at all, and meanwhile the fish tank still sits there, occupying ground needed for a number of other plants that desperately need to be set out.

Gardeners know that these anxieties are inherent and will not be escaped for long in any season, but especially in spring.

In the middle of everything my crinum bulbs arrived from Georgia. What a bright spot to see such superb plants. They were set out in a downpour. As they begin to grow they will need a two-inch mulch and heavy watering every week or so through the summer, stopping the water a little before Labor Day, and a six-inch mulch in November.

The tree peonies, which recently provided two days of supreme beauty before they were ruined by the weather, grow against a raised pool and must be examined frequently to make sure little strands of honeysuckle, akebia, bindweed, or polygonum have not started creeping in beneath their dense glaucous canopy. Once such intruders have a foothold, it is agonizing to get them out without damaging the peony branches. The gardener tending to such donkey tasks must keep clearly in mind the image of the plants loaded with dinner-plate flowers of coral, blush, and royal purple (which he sees in most years for a full five or six days).

As I watched *Nightline* on television, it suddenly struck me that the moonflower vines have not yet been planted. The seeds should have gone in the first of May. That program specializes in things to worry about and often reminds me of dreadful deficiencies in the garden.

Now that the sun is supposed to come out again, it appears the roses have been gaining strength (and not rotting, as one's gloomy forebodings suggested), and frankly there is some triumph in having 'Aglaia' blooming over an arch. All the best writers say it is not worth growing, being "pale and ineffectual," so naturally it was a rose I had to have. Admittedly it did not bloom for two years, but now it is a mass of primrose fading to white, far more delicate and refined than 'Goldfinch' and with a finer scent and glossier, more elegant foliage. Of course it is pale if it's primrose fading to white, and if you want purple and gold it will not do at all. It is a child of the old noisette rose 'Rêve d'Or'.

'Aglaia' should not be recommended to anybody, necessarily, and it never is. The flowers in small clusters are an inch and a half wide with perhaps twenty-five small petals and a brush of orange-gold stamens in the middle of the shallow saucer. It has only one flush of bloom, and possibly small gardeners would do better to give an arch to a rose that blooms off and on through the summer. Still, 'Aglaia' is an "important" rose, as ancestor of the so-called hybrid musks. Besides, whenever I hear some flower dismissed as relatively worthless I am seized with an urge to grow it.

Brave Spikes of Flowers

GARDENERS ARE VAGUE if you ask them how long certain plants bloom, usually erring on the generous side. This is partly the result of English books, in which an endless number of plants are said to flower from "June to September," and even when they are specific they are misleading to gardeners here.

One of my favorite lists is one of the times at which various rambler roses bloom. I was so pleased to discover it in an English book of 1910, as few modern books even acknowledge that such roses exist. The point of that list was to help the gardener choose roses that bloomed at the same time or to arrange for a succession of flowers over a period of three months.

In Washington, however, all the ramblers and climbers bloom in May and that's that, except for the ones that bloom feebly now and then until frost. They vary by a few days, of course, but with me they all overlap. Most of them are in showy bloom for ten days rather than the "six weeks" promised in various foreign texts.

Tall bearded irises in the average garden are in showy bloom for two weeks. Their season may last six weeks, but most of them bloom at midseason, and each clump, on average, is in flower for two weeks. Early and late varieties extend the season, and iris fanciers often get a foretaste of the main show by planting "intermediates," those irises with flower stems usually less than twenty-seven inches high, which as a group bloom in late April. There are even earlier irises, the various dwarf bearded varieties, up to a foot high, and some dwarf beardless irises (such as the species *reticulata*) that bloom in March.

When I grew several hundred kinds of tall May-flowering irises, we allowed two weeks from the time the leaves showed swelling flower stalks until they reached full height and flowered, then counted on two weeks of actual bloom. When the blooming season was over in early June, hardly any of us fanatics wished it a day longer.

Gardeners keen to grow the earliest tall irises and also the latest (as indicated in iris catalogues) may group the quite early and quite late varieties in separate beds so they make a nice show. Gardeners who do not go berserk for irises, however, but grow only a few clumps, need not concern themselves much about the time of bloom.

But in a large planting it is dismal to see brave spikes of flower at a peak of vigor, surrounded by hundreds of stems with the last bloom hanging on.

Another thing: irises will give far more pleasure if every day the fading blooms are snapped off. It can be done quickly, even in a garden with hundreds of varieties, and the gardener will enjoy visiting the flowers closely.

A plant deserving far more attention than it is usually given is the Spanish scilla or bluebell. We have friends who call them English bluebells (which they are not — that bluebell is *Scilla nutans* and it is not as garden-worthy), but the plant I mean is usually listed in catalogues or labeled in garden shops as *Scilla campanulata*. Sometimes it is called *Endymion hispanicus,* thanks to pesky botanists whose great aim in life is to change plant names.

These flowers bridge the little gap between tulip and iris times.

They are not only permanent, lasting for decades in gardens (perhaps centuries?), but also increase, which is not true of many first-class flowers.

The stems are a foot or so (once a batch of the blue variety 'Excelsior' reached twenty-two inches), hung with a dozen or more trumpet-bell flowers along the top third of the stem. The handsomest are the lavender-blues, but there are white and rose-colored kinds that are probably just as beautiful, except that like most gardeners I fall over myself for blue flowers.

These scillas last in flower for three weeks and do not look bad afterward. Bulbs are planted in October, and they are, as things go, cheap. If you plant them in front of azaleas — a very good place for them, as they endure but do not require shade — you will have to transplant them every few years as the azaleas spread out. I have some scillas, snowdrops, trout lilies, and, I fear, a few other things that are now three feet back beneath azalea branches. The bulbs should be dug up and planted where they get some light. This should have been a project four years ago.

The Best-Laid Plants

❀ YOU HAVE A CHOICE, when your carefully thought out plans for summer flowers all fail, either to sulk and surrender the garden to bindweed or to say all is not lost: though much is a ruin, much remains.

I am rather an expert at this. There is a space of twenty feet between the large fishpool and the small tank, and here I proposed a carpet of the semiwild petunias you find along alleys, with twenty or so plants of the elegant wild green nicotiana, *N. langsdorffii,* and at each end of the two beds a standard brugmansia, with big hanging trumpets of yellow and white.

The first setback was the death of three of the brugmansias over winter. Then, for some odd reason, not a single self-sown petunia has appeared along our alley, though usually there are hundreds. Besides all that, not a single plant resulted from sowing two packets of the nicotiana in sterilized soil in the best way. Also, not one seedling has appeared from the giant *N. sylvestris* that I always count on — a few little plants always pop up from last year's plant, usually right at the edge of a pavement.

You will see that the original plan, therefore, has had to be modified somewhat. Over my dead body I have acquired twenty plants of those modern petunias I dislike, white edged with red and white edged with rose. And instead of the green nicotianas I am settling for twenty plants of annual pinks and carnations. It is all a pain in the neck.

Elsewhere I was counting heavily on a mass of white cleomes, though not one plant has come up from a large amount of seed sown.

In another place there were to be a dozen or so white sunflowers, accented by several orange-red tithonias. The sunflowers at least have come up like mustard, though from a large planting of tithonia seed only two plants have appeared.

Fortunately I now have several good young plants of the American four-o'clock, the one with trumpets thin as quills and said to be highly perfumed at night.

To quote one of our fine poets, now we see how vain it was to boast of fleeting things so certain to be lost. We do what we can with what we have. Many fine gardens present themselves to admiring eyes in summer with virtually none of the originally planned flowers present. Gardening is no job for rigid people who must follow the drill set down in January.

I do feel the percentage of failure for my summer flowers is higher than seems fair. Note that, ye garden gods.

On the other hand, my wild cannas survived the winter well in a plastic trash bag, and in addition I have two young plants, both looking in top shape, ready to take on the world, of the very tall, very elegant *Canna iridiflora*.

Also, at the moment the rather despised turn-of-the-century rambler 'Aglaia', is showing itself to be a delicate mass of yellow-white roses, and the striped white and purple-red, intensely scented 'Variegata di Bologna' has wandered fifteen or twenty feet into a yew tree, and its striking flowers nod down in a perfect way.

Things even out. Or even if they don't quite, we make do with what survives and flourishes and (once some private whining has been gotten over) are thankful.

Where Iris Is, I'm Smiling

EVERYTHING IS RELATIVE — certainly color is. An iris I am glad to see again is 'Alta California', which came out in 1931. Not so long ago, but as irises go an antique. When I first saw it in 1932, this iris was thought a marvel, as indeed it was. Never before had we seen an iris of large size, yellow, tall, and superbly branched. After a few years I was able to acquire it and for some years I grew it, but as the decades passed so did the iris.

Several years ago I alluded to it, and a generous reader, who has since died, offered me a plant, which he had grown ever since he bought it when it was new. How he happened to keep it for sixty years I do not know.

I expected to see it as I remembered it from boyhood, a light yellow self, near the color of sulfur. Instead, the standards or top petals were and are a subdued lemon and the falls are buff, clouded with a tan overlay, and at their base are many brown striations. Thus the memory often fails the gardener.

Viewed from a few feet, 'Alta California' still looks all yellow, very soft, almost a bright straw color, and this is the tone of yellow that is so valuable in an iris border, blending perfectly with blue, lavender, rose, raspberry, and almost everything else, though a more saturated and stronger yellow looks better with dark blue and purple.

Most irises old and new have indifferent branching; that is, the bloom stalk has short spurs along the side bearing flowers. A few, like this old one I speak of, have curved branches of considerable length, carrying the side flowers as much as eight inches from the main stalk.

However much I treasure this variety, I would never recommend it to anybody else, as there are dozens of newer varieties of clearer color, more flaring falls, wider petals with more ruffling, and so on.

At one point I made a collection of irises that adorned gardens before the late 1920s, when the great white 'Purissima' came out and changed garden irises for the better. The old irises as a group have smaller fans of leaves and therefore more bloom stalks per square yard. The flowers are often smaller than modern kinds. Unfortunately they are equally susceptible to rot and to borers, in my experience, and as their colors are less sparkling, there is not much reason to grow them except for historical or sentimental interest.

An hour's walk in my neighborhood showed a good fifteen varieties of old-timers in the yards, and often only one variety was grown in each. Sometimes three houses in a row had the same iris, so I imagine they were passed around.

The great season for tall bearded irises begins in late April and early May in places such as northern Mississippi, two weeks later in Washington, and progressively later farther north. Fortunately irises have not lost their fragrance through many generations of breeding, and every iris grower knows and revels in the variety of scents. Some are like sweet peas, some like ripe grapes, and some have an indefinable sweetness not like anything else.

The time to plant the rhizomes, which are storage roots like small sweet potatoes, is from July through September, though they can be moved anytime if necessary. If, for example, the gardener is moving and cannot bear to leave a particular variety, it can be dug up any month of the year in climates like that of Washington.

They like full sun. They bloom magnificently in slight shade, with six hours of sun a day, but not so freely as in full sun. They like rich soil, preferably a sandy loam, though clay loam, even acid clay loam, does perfectly well provided water does not stand on the plants for hours after a rain. They greatly like rotted manure, which is dangerous, as the resulting lush growth is more liable to rot than irises on leaner diets.

The most spectacular irises I ever grew followed a mulch of almost fresh manure one January. Another and safer road to particularly fine irises is the use of massive amounts of pure leaf mold.

They do not need protection in winter, though a certain number of bloom stalks will be lost every year from late freezes in spring, just as the flower stalks come through the earth inside the leaf fans.

Some gardeners have had good results with heavy mulches of wood chips. Sometimes these not only protect emerging bloom stalks but also make it harder for the iris borer to establish itself. One gardener who had astonishingly large, fine irises mulched the entire planting with about six inches of sugar cane waste. I foretold dreadful rot, but there was no rot.

It's often said that irises have shallow roots, and so they do if the earth is dug ten or twelve inches before planting. But if the iris bed is dug forty inches (surely some bravado here?) the iris roots will go down forty inches. I have seen them. A foot or twenty inches is less backbreaking and does well enough.

Rather than mulches, a safer course is continual cultivation, but that is endless labor and few will attempt it. If, however, the gardener has many grudges and an old butcher knife with the bottom inch or two broken off, spectacular results can be achieved by stabbing straight down two inches over the entire planting. This is repeated about every two weeks through the growing season.

Beginners can hardly do better than to choose from the collections offered by large iris nurseries, usually one rhizome each of say ten or fifteen varieties in different colors. They come with names attached, and one should keep a record of the names, as within a year or two one would very much like the name of some particular iris, even though at the time of planting the gardener didn't care what the names were and merely wanted an assortment of fine colors.

The spring after planting there will usually be one bloom stalk, and the second year there will be five, say, and in the third year perhaps ten or twelve. They are best dug up after the third year, divided and replanted using three young vigorous rhizomes set a foot apart in a triangle, the fans all pointing the same direction. (There will be many extra rhizomes, which can be planted elsewhere or given away.) The danger of growing a few irises is that the gardener will start chopping up the lawn for additional space for irises, and then the daylilies, roses, and everything else will be dug out to make room for yet more. Within ten years, however, a few other plants will be allowed back.

Rosy Outlook

✳ THE MOST OVERPOWERING TIME of year in my garden is when the rambler and climbing roses bloom. Not even azaleas, not even masses of tall bearded irises, produce such a sense of opulence, and this is no doubt because the masses of bloom are borne from ground level to fifteen feet in the air.

Also, unexpected combinations of color appear as you walk about the garden, thus seeing different roses as the perspective changes. The best time of day is eight or nine in the morning or after five-thirty in the afternoon. Few flowers look their best in the heat of the day, and roses are no exception.

I am quite satisfied as I walk the hundred or so feet from the kitchen to the alley. First, to the left is a bush of the rugosa rose 'Belle Poitevine', a fragrant blowsy pink bush with a good bit of blue in the rose color. Just ahead and nearer the walk is a twelve-foot-high bush of the rugosa 'Mrs. Anthony Waterer', bred from the highly perfumed old hybrid perpetual 'Général Jacqueminot', as fragrant as its parent. At its full height it leans into a fragrant white rambler, 'Seagull', which clothes an arch over the walk. A few feet beyond is the nineteenth-century creamy white, fragrant rambler 'Aglaia', with the scentless purple rambler 'Violette' growing into it from the other side. The white is almost finished before the purple blooms. Their flowering overlaps only a few days.

'Aglaia' has clusters of double flowers that open all together in such a mass that the leaves are hidden, as is true of most old ramblers. But 'Seagull' opens its semidouble clusters of inch-wide dead white flowers little by little, giving a starry-night effect for several days until the whole plant is solid white.

Beyond, on either side of the walk, are fat bushes about seven feet high of the white hybrid musk 'Moonlight', which blooms off and on till frost. To the sides, thirty feet off, is the large-flowered climber 'Madame Grégoire Staechelin', with ruffled, perfumed flowers showing a deeper rose on the reverse of the petals.

Next there is another arch with 'Blairii No. 2' on it. This is an old Bourbon rose that should not be on a small arch over a walk but should be given a stout post to grow on, with room to spread out. Its medium pink, fragrant petals are jammed into a circle, and the outer rim is almost white. The rambler 'Violette' grows on the other side of the arch and mingles with it.

Beyond is a final arch with the single scentless bush rose 'Mutabilis' on one side and a great swag of 'Seagull' on the other, drooping over from its position in a tall yew.

The other side of the yew is support for 'Mrs. F. W. Flight', a scented pink rambler that has large clusters of semidouble flowers. It is the pink rose grown on the tall pylons at the Roseraie de l'Haÿ outside of Paris.

After the last arch is the modern climber 'Blossomtime', with hybrid tea–type blooms of pink, the outer petals paler. It has the good habit of casting its fragrance, and it blooms till November off and on.

On some timbers across the walk is the old noisette rose 'Jaune Desprez', which was offered about 1830 as the first yellow climber, but in our springs it is pinkish apricot with a touch of orange. It is intensely fragrant, and beyond it is the old rambler 'The Garland', with unbelievable masses of small white perfumed flowers in great clusters.

To one side, tangling with it, is the Bourbon 'Variegata di Bologna', extremely double and intensely scented light pink blooms striped with crimson-purple. It grows into the white rambler and on into a red cedar.

Some of these roses are popular, at least in famous gardens, and others not. To the extreme left of these is a white multiflora rambler that you might think is the wild *Rosa multiflora*, but my friend Nicholas Weber points out various differences. It has the overwhelming fragrance of the multiflora and came from the garden of the late Mrs. Frederick Keays in Maryland, the woman who did much to start the interest in old roses decades ago.

Far to the right against a fence is 'Polyantha Grandiflora', a larger, glossier variant on the multiflora, and running in back of it are the white 'Madame Plantier' and some albas.

Most of these roses bloom only in spring and only for a couple of weeks. When they bloom I feel I have all the roses I want, so massive is their flowering. I may have missed a few along the way: the yellow, strangely scented 'Agnes', deep red 'Dr. Huey', the perfumed pink rambler 'Ginny', the barely scented scarlet 'Will Scarlet'. It might be more tasteful to have less of this mass flowering, but if you want to feel drowned in roses, these are the kinds that will do it.

When the sun shines and nothing dreadful is happening at the moment all losses are restored.

June

The Ivy League

ONCE A GARDENER has some plant he once longed for, he takes it for granted. It is somewhat like sex — the mad excitement cannot be expected to last.

Yesterday I was sitting outdoors in the open summerhouse in the curvy iron chair on the pavement of bricks, and the light was that incomparable light that filters through leaves of the grapevine overhead. The summerhouse backs up to the main house, and at the base of the house wall is a strip of earth eighteen inches wide planted with the yellow ivy 'Buttercup' and the glossy Persian ivy *Hedera colchica*. After three years the glossy ivy has decided to climb the house wall.

Each of these things — the ivies, the grape, the summerhouse itself, the brick pavement — was once an urgent passion, and I had anxieties and fits until each of them was built or planted. Even now, if I think directly about any of these things, I remember with delight the days when I built this or planted that, sometimes after a long search or a long session with graph paper before the thing was accomplished.

But now contentment replaces the anxiety, the excitement, the impatience, and at this rate I'll be turning into one of those Chinese sages who, at the age of ninety or so, can do whatever they like without any qualm.

So there I was, sitting under the grapevine at the large iron table (recently painted black, and what a good job, I thought with some smugness) with a box of new plants that required potting.

The weather was, for a change, glorious. Fear no more the heat of the sun, I said, reaching for a strange little creeping fig. The regular creeping fig is not quite hardy in Washington but will survive against a wall with some winter protection and a bit of luck. But there is also a form with white-variegated leaves and another one with leaves like a tiny oak.

The grower sent a note apologizing for the blue-flowered clerodendrum from Uganda, "such beautiful flowers but an ugly plant," yet I thought the plant quite a nice one, about ten inches high, and I expect it to bloom by the end of the millennium.

Then I got four plants of the night jasmine. All are gone now, given away in small fits of enthusiasm. I miss them already. Gardeners can be Indian givers at heart.

A weak bronze-leaved variety of New Zealand flax, *Phormium tenax,* promises several years of anxious futzing about with pots until it is at last sturdy enough to go outdoors, at which point it will probably die the first winter. Phormiums do, but the gardener is convinced if he keeps trying he'll find one that's hardy to winter cold.

For years I have sought the kind of yellow swamp iris, *Iris pseudacorus,* with brilliant gold leaves when it sprouts in the spring, which turn gradually to green in July. There is a good one from Germany that I found at a garden center in London, but once all its leaves and all its roots were cut off and the rhizome scrubbed, it was too weak to make it through the first Washington summer.

Finally I found the variegated kind listed in an old catalogue of Glasshouse Works, in Stewart, Ohio. They said it was not listed in this year's catalogue and they had only small plants newly potted, but they sold me two of them. What a pleasure to get them into their new pot, watered heavily, to be shaded for some days in the soft light beneath the grape.

There is also a kind of wild Japanese iris with occasional solid white leaves, called *Iris ensata spontanea variegata.* It keeps the white all summer and fall. The flowers will be small and far from the opulent fat blooms of garden varieties, but the occasional white leaves make a clump unusual and eye-catching.

The best way to handle Japanese irises (which used to be called *I. kaempferi,* now *ensata*) is to stand the pot in a saucer that holds one to two inches of water all the time. Of course they do not need to be grown in pots but are quite happy planted in the garden like any other perennial, only in a sunny damp spot, avoiding any trace of lime in the soil. I grow this one in a pot only because I want to keep an eye on it.

Unfortunately, the Japanese irises can get rhizome borers, just as the tall bearded and Siberian irises do. I have had borers in all of them. There are poisons to keep the borers out, but as I do not use them, my iris sufferings have been substantial.

Still, as I went about my potting on a glorious afternoon, one small treasure after another, the world of nature that is so terrible and so beautiful appeared only in its sweetest aspect. From this same vantage point in the summerhouse I once saw a grackle seize and fly off with a baby sparrow. And I well know gardeners are not idiots, or at least not because we garden, and no class of folk is more keenly aware how shaky the world is and how quickly the big sun is obscured and storms batter the frail erigerons that would have been strong enough in another two weeks, and so on endlessly.

All the same, it's true that when the sun shines and nothing dreadful is happening at the moment, at least not within sight or consciousness, all losses, as the great wit of the language once observed, are restored and sorrows end.

Fare of the Dog

✾ SEED OF MY WHITE SUNFLOWER sprouted well in a pot twelve inches wide, and small plants were thinned out to fill another large pot before reaching a size great enough to withstand the rough life of the open garden.

It baffled me that suddenly the leaves seemed so severely chewed as to threaten the life of the young sunflowers. This past week I discovered that Maud, the mongrel of complex terrier ancestry, was not only chewing the leaves but swallowing them.

A friend who is given to theories of conspiracy and who thinks all crime is related to drugs said there is some narcotic in sunflower leaves, but I think Maud simply likes the flavor. I have now planted what remains of these young plants in the open garden and hope she will leave them alone.

During the winter she chewed off leaves of the fiddle-leaf fig and dropped them in the living room. She did not eat them but made a few tooth marks. The joy, apparently, was to pull them off.

Most dogs, I believe, like to graze to a small extent in the garden, and I believe their preferences are arbitrary, varying from beast to beast, for no reason in particular.

Jack, a Welsh terrier of my boyhood, was interested in only two plants. He pulled off and ate gardenia flowers, and he fancied a white water lily, 'Gonnere'. He swam out into the fish pool, got the stem in his mouth, and pulled, swimming to shore with his trophy. He chewed on the flower a bit, then left the mangled remains on the grass. He was not interested in any other water lily, and when ashore he cared for no flower except the gardenia.

A basset hound, Bass, ate very little vegetable matter except pecans. She would deposit perhaps ten of the nuts in the shell on a daybed in a room off the back hall and at leisure would crack them to extract every particle of nutmeat but never ate the bitter membrane. She is the only dog we ever heard of who was expert at pecanery, and I still have no understanding of how her relatively large, blunt teeth could accomplish the work.

The only other garden thing she ate was lettuce. On numerous occasions she stole a head of lettuce from a grocery bag and devoured it quietly on the same daybed. She also ate several thousand cicadas during their brief but massive appearance in 1970. We kept count.

Ginger is not a garden vegetable, but once she ate three pounds of candied ginger in one afternoon, the entire contents of a large box sent by my mother-in-law. She also once ate thirty-six vanilla muffins fresh from the oven, but that hardly counts.

Another basset, Luke, ate a grand total of one cicada, as far as we could tell. He did not eat lettuce but ate cabbage. He made so much noise that he rarely got very far, as he could be heard through much of the house, and his delight was therefore usually interrupted. We thought he might have learned about cabbage from a leopard tortoise, Pilgrim, who ate one head of cabbage (among other dainties) a week. Luke is the only dog we ever had who got drunk. He licked the remnants of fifty cups of eggnog after a party. The vet said there was nothing to do but leave him alone, and after a day and a half on his back with his paws up, and considerable groaning, he seemed as good as new.

A third basset some years later ate very little in the garden except blueberries. As you know, these turn blue before they are fully ripe, but she discovered that when they were dead ripe and at maximum sweetness, she could run her tongue along the twigs, applying a certain pressure. The truly ripe ones came off, but the rest, even when fully colored, stayed on the bushes.

One year for several days she licked seedpods of the opium poppies if they had that latex-type exudate, but we saw no sign of intoxication.

The greatest eater we had was Max, a Welsh terrier. He once chewed a number of dormant rose bushes in February, soon after they had been planted. Thorns he avoided or else did not mind. His triumph was to chew all the way through a magnificent clematis vine with a stem as thick as a broomstick. He also loved all members of the cabbage family. Once he got all four paws (and the rest of him, of course) into a large crock of shredded cabbage for sauerkraut. I thought no harm was done, as the cabbage would ferment and be wholesome, but my wife would not hear of it and threw all the cabbage out. His greatest passion was for Brussels sprouts, but only when cooked. The smell always brought him flying. He did not bother such herbs as basil and sage, but he was so fond of dill that we never had any for the house while he lived, though we kept planting it. He liked to climb into the long wooden box where it was sown and trot down its length, eating as he went.

No dog we ever had liked nasturtiums or, as far as we know, ever tried them, which is surprising, as they are more edible than rose stems or sunflower leaves or seeds (which Maud also eats).

More damage is done, as a rule, by dogs' sitting on young plants or romping through them than by their ingesting them. The losses are minor and rarely make any difference, except the dill, and in any case, if you are going to have the sparkling dog about the place, you can expect a certain amount of gustatory exploration. Otherwise, if it upsets the gardener, he can settle for a ceramic cat.

How Does Your Garden Grow?
Any Way You Choose

GARDENS ARE LIKE people's lives: they aim at different goals, all more or less legitimate. But this means a superb garden of one type will draw only blank astonishment from a gardener whose plot is of another type.

Gertrude Jekyll, the eminent Edwardian gardener, designed her garden to "paint pictures" with living plants. She thought of it as a landscape in three dimensions, but with color and shapes used as a painter might use them.

André Lenôtre, the great French gardener of the seventeenth century, thought a garden should be a background for court ceremonial and should therefore have fabulously wide spaces for promenades and plenty of fountains as well as smooth reflecting pools.

E. A. Bowles, a great English gardener, thought the garden should be a collection of favorite plants, including oddities valued only for themselves and that did not count at all in the general picture.

Some gardens aim at neat, orderly surroundings to a house, in which the garden looks good throughout the year, preferably with little labor needed. Such a garden relies on masses of green, plenty of paving, interesting textures, but with no attention given to flowering plants except as incidentals.

Others strive to reproduce a natural woodland or meadow, sometimes enriching a natural landscape with native or even exotic plants. Thus a small woodland may look wild and untouched, but with clumps of lilies not originally found in it, and perhaps drifts of daffodils and fall crocuses that would never be in that woodland unless planted by man.

Or a seemingly natural meadow could be made more flowery by introducing cornflowers, poppies, butterfly weed, buddleia, various California wildflowers, wild tulips from Asia Minor, and so forth. The meadow would still look wild but would have a great deal more color than an untouched meadow would ever have.

A water garden might consist of great rectangular pools set with masonry copings, or the water might be designed to look like a woodland pond overhung with willows. In each case there might be scarlet goldfish and water lilies of red, yellow, or blue, none of which would ever be found in a truly wild pond of that particular region.

A quite pretty garden could be an orchard, with the trees not too closely spaced, and beneath there might be a meadow garden packed with bright flowers from bulbs and other exotic — that is, nonnative — plants.

Popular now is the cottage garden, in which small trees, bulbs, roses, old-fashioned flowers (foxgloves, hollyhocks, larkspurs, valerian, and so on), and perhaps tomatoes, beans, and cabbages are all planted seemingly at random.

Quite apart from all these kinds of gardens based on different aesthetics and different ways of living, gardens even within one category will vary depending on the owner's wallet and his idea of what the garden means to him. A garden with a maintenance budget of $150 a year may differ astonishingly from one on which $4,000 a year is spent, even though both gardens are the same type, even of the same design.

In my own garden I have no paid labor. I do it all myself. This is partly because I am tight with money, partly because I am not rich, but mostly because I don't like other people pawing over my treasures.

My approach would never do if the aim were to view the garden as a painted landscape or a composition of geometric forms. My garden will always be a cottage garden, though with some slight attention to mass effects (on a small scale). It will always give preference to plants over anything else. In back of all that is my personal view (no better or worse than dozens of other gardening views) that the place is so personal I cannot even hire anybody to weed or trim shrubs or sweep bricks or set tiles in the raised walls of a fish pool or build a shed or a summerhouse.

I well know I have neither the time nor the energy nor even the desire to have a garden that people admire. It is not for them but for me. I attach far more importance to the progress of the plants — the cycle of growth and decay — than to the floral display of the moment or to the effects of open space. If I want a few tiger lilies, as I certainly do, and if the best site for them happens to be beside a crimson shrub rose, then that's where they go.

My daylilies are almost all yellow or pastel melon colors, but if I happen to love a six-foot-tall wild daylily like *Hemerocallis altissima,* I do not hesitate to include it, and the same goes for the night-blooming wild *H. citrina,* which looks sad all day long.

Whatever the underlying philosophy happens to be, almost every gardener will pay some attention to contrasts of texture and color and will give some thought to the aesthetic effect of paths and benches and sheds.

Gardens are not quite so different from one another as you might think at first. Even Versailles has some attractive plants in it, and even a jumble of marigolds, petunias, cleomes, chicory, tomatoes, and onions presided over by a fig tree against a shack — even in such a garden there is often a degree of self-conscious attention paid to the aesthetics of the arrangement.

As long as there are plants at all, and as long as the gardener is human, and as long as the garden is an important part of the gardener's leisure, there will be a bond or a spirit between all gardens of whatever type.

The Computer as Gardener's Friend

NOTHING IN THE YEAR is more splendid than a week in the nineties, a trifle uncomfortable in the afternoon but glorious at five in the morning.

Even in my wretched patch it is a joy to see the fragile poppies open, the mass of nasturtiums growing in a tub and a box. I pick them every other day if I don't forget them, and it is extraordinary how freely they bloom. The 'Gleam Hybrids' are not as good as the old original 'Scarlet Gleam', by the way, but the color range is wider, including buff and a kind of fawn color.

It is worth the trouble to give moonflower vines a good bucket of water every day. This makes the difference between a struggling plant and one leaping twenty-five feet into the air. On wires or other support, of course.

How remarkable that now the variegated yucca is in bloom, the flowers are thick with a tiny brown beetle with black head and rump. They spend most of the day copulating on the waxy petals, but when they tire of that they crawl, somewhat aimlessly, about the petals without much sense of direction and very little clue where the nectar is. I have never seen them in the garden before — consider how complex the mechanism is that draws them from who knows where when the yucca blooms.

Sometimes one is baffled by a vine, wishing to lead it across some open space and not sure of the best way. I find that computer cable, dark gray in color, is admirable. A leading occupation in most offices is getting rid of old computers and installing new systems. Often one can find a whole garbage can of computer cable being thrown out. At one place I have used a catenary (which is simply the natural arc a rope or chain falls into when suspended between two posts) of this cable to lead a pink clematis (sometimes called *C. spooneri rosea* and sometimes *C. vedrariensis*) away from one column to another. I do not like to see any structural post smothered with vines, and try to keep mine clean enough that the post can be seen at side and top, even if I have allowed a vine to grow up it.

This rubber- or plastic-covered wire, about as thick as a pencil, is also useful for tying up a vertical yew or box that wants to spread. Winter snow usually spreads out the branches, ruining the tight vertical look, but not if the branches are roped in. A simple knot (preferably at the back of the plant, where it is less noticeable) holds it together — nothing elaborate is needed.

Once a man from the telephone company gave me a lot of scrap insulated wire left over from a job. Unfortunately it was dead white, and you have to be pretty clever to tie in your branches without the glaring white wire being visible. So one good thing I say about computers is that they produce for gardeners a lot of usable cable, and the more they rip them out the better I like it.

The Hard Way, Firmly Planted

❀ ONE INTERESTING THING about technology is that when it comes to pleasant living, it delivers less than is advertised. We do not yet, for example, have reliable general-purpose garden weed-killers nor, for that matter, garden hoses as good as they used to be. In the garden, technology seems to mean plastic watering cans instead of copper ones, lumber that is less than its stated dimensions, flimsy stakes, flimsy trellises, tiny packets of fertilizer at amazing prices, and no stable manure.

I do not necessarily want to return to the days that are past, but I do rather fail to see that technology has done anything for my own garden to speak of. Things like irises have to be hand-weeded, and nothing is more labor than a rock garden, but I don't see gardeners giving up things like that. Many a gardener raises vegetables that require intensive hand labor and involve a cost hardly justified by the harvest.

Gardeners know that. They are not fools and they are not blind. But even if your own string beans do not taste any better than those from the supermarket, there is a satisfaction from growing your own that is hardly equaled by standing in line at any checkout counter.

People like gardening precisely because it differs from the "efficiency" of modern life. People like to dig, and they like to dig with the same spade or fork that their predecessors used a thousand years before them.

They like to tie up grapevines. They like to prune great climbing roses. They like to stake lilies. I once had 2,500 bloom stalks of irises in May and 250 stakes that I moved about as needed. I quite enjoyed staking the irises, because the idea was not to save time but to gaze at each stalk one by one, and of the perhaps 20,000 iris flowers that year, not one opened and not one faded but I noticed it and, while it was in bloom, gazed at it.

Gardeners are so little interested in being sensible that they grow vast quantities of plants that are not nearly as handsome as other varieties they might just as easily have. I like *Astrantia major,* with wiry stems and flowers not much bigger than a quarter. They are greenish off-white and off-pink. They look like nothing much when in full bloom, but I like them.

I keep puttering about with the wild *Iris cristata,* which blooms two inches off the ground. If I grew it in a vast fat clump in the border, it would make rather a show for a week, but I grow it in cracks between huge maple roots. Sometimes the dogs uproot it, or the squirrels (its roots are scanty and right at the surface, and it doesn't take much to uproot it), and in such an unfavorable site I need not expect it to perform terribly well. Still, there it is.

Then I have one mountain laurel on a dry bank. It would do better, of course, in a sort of glade with deep leaf mold, but the spots it would like best are occupied by azaleas, nandinas, and other creatures, so it abides the dry bank. I have to carry buckets of water to it from time to time. It is there because I want it there, and for no more sensible reason.

How many of us have oddments tucked in here and there that make no real show when they bloom and that often enough require special care, since they are not in the best positions for their growth.

It would be interesting to know how many gardeners here plant delphiniums year by year, knowing they are not going to grow very well, if indeed they don't die out They are as pleased with a few scrawny stalks as if they had a forest of stems six feet high laden with flowers of Chelsea show standard.

This year I have two sweet peas growing in a tub where they compete with a flourishing (I am happy to say) tomato. I expect to reap a tremendous harvest of perhaps twelve blooms in June. That would not make even one vase, even if they all came at once. So it is hardly worth doing, yet I would be no end annoyed if anything happened to the feeble vines (which I started in individual pots in late winter in the house and fidgeted with considerably until they were planted out in March, which was too early, as it turned out).

No, efficiency and practicality do not have much to do with the small town garden, I am afraid — or, rather, I am delighted to report. There are probably only about a hundred million Americans at the moment who understand this.

Contemplating Small Illusions

IF YOU STEP OFF twenty by forty feet outdoors and mark the boundaries with stakes, you will be distressed how small it looks. If you come indoors and measure a room twenty by forty feet, you will be surprised how large it is.

Now gardens are largely outdoor phenomena, with the result that they look small, but they look vastly larger when enclosed with walls. Of course we may not want walls, or may not be able to pay for them, or may not be allowed to erect them for zoning reasons; but the point remains, any enclosure will give an effect of greater space.

I do not want my small town garden to pretend to be Versailles, and I see no good reason to try to disguise its small size. All the same, I would like it to seem roomy and comfortable, and without disguising its size in any silly way, this may be accomplished by dividing the garden, however small, into smaller pieces.

If the small garden is entered from the back of the house, it may be feasible to run a row of posts parallel to the house with vines on them, and pave the space between the house wall and the posts. This may provide a pleasant effect even if the space is only six feet wide. You would sit on the paved terrace and look through the vine-covered posts. The effect will be a good bit more spacious than if the posts were not there.

In plain fact you have reduced the size of the garden by giving six feet to pavement and posts, but the eye interprets this as an increase in garden size.

Another way of dividing the garden is by changing the level. Suppose it is flat. A third of the garden may be raised twenty inches higher than the rest, reached by steps. However simple-minded this may seem, it can be effective.

Here, just let me urge the most valuable of hints: before you do any dividing of the garden at all, test it out by temporarily setting up poles or baffles (four-by-eight pieces of plywood) to see if you like the effect.

Another thing: be careful about steps. In the garden they are almost always too narrow. The steps should have shallow risers, say four inches. The treads may be quite deep. You are not designing functional ways to get to the attic, after all, but are trying to create an effect of space and serenity.

Sometimes it is a terrible problem what to do with earth excavated to form a lily pool. It could be used to make a slight change of grade. Even if it is only a foot, a flight of three steps up can make it visually important.

Often in cities the garden is a long narrow rectangle. If the view to begin with is between a couple of tree trunks or columns or posts with vines, the first impact may be pleasanter than with an unobstructed view.

Beyond that, maybe a third of the way down the garden length, there may easily be another partial visual barrier. You do not, of course, want to cut the garden into tiny sealed-in rooms, but partial barriers that you see through or see around easily may give the illusion of distance or space, just as you find inside a house where one room opens into another.

Hedges of low height (two to four feet) may sometimes be right. Again, a hedge of yew or beautiful common red cedar may reach out into the garden from the side boundary, not running all the way across the garden but only a few feet. While not really concealing the long boundary of the garden, such right-angle short hedges may do much to obliterate the sense of a constraining and too-narrow rectangle.

Or perhaps the garden is meant to look informal, and yew hedges strike you as all wrong for the effect you want. The principle can still hold of reaching into the garden from its long boundaries to break up the long view of the boundary fence. Instead of clipped hedges, you could use an unclipped informal shrub. A good one is the flat-tiered viburnum, such as *V. plicatum tomentosum* or one of its garden varieties such as 'Mariesii'. Varieties of American holly (or English or Chinese) make substantial visual accents, and of course may be grown unclipped.

Some gardeners have found, in small narrow gardens, that they like the effect of brilliant colors near at hand. Thus the scarlet zinnias, or azaleas, or neon-orange daylilies would be planted nearest the house and softer colors would be set farther off, so that at the extreme far end there would be gray and soft blue and straw-yellow.

Until the gardener experiments a bit, he has little idea how a long narrow plot can be changed simply by dividing the garden into three or four parts by means of partial hedges, by open screens of posts with vines, or large shrubs with openings between them for the eye to see into the distance.

Heeding the Garden's Call of the Wild

OFTEN THERE ARE SLIGHT VARIATIONS in plants that make a difference to gardeners. It is well worth keeping one's eyes open for the oddities. Sometimes they are worth growing simply because they are odd, but sometimes they are more beautiful or have some other great advantage.

I was told by a daughter of a famous plant collector that some of her mother's happy discoveries were made when they stopped for gas. When you read that such-and-such was collected in the remote river country of some far-off place, you assume the collector climbed cliffs, but sometimes there was no such difficulty.

I recall seeing a wild American phlox that looked like all the others, but it had an intense perfume of heliotrope. Why? Nobody knows, it just did.

In our alley I used to admire a sprig of the porcelain berry that had leaves beautifully silvered, with just enough green to provide the chlorophyll of life. This was *Ampelopsis brevipedunculata,* and the variegated silver form is usually called *elegans.* You see it offered for sale sometimes, but you also see it occasionally as just one twig on an otherwise green plant. If cuttings are made of the silver form, the whole plant will be silver.

This is a beautiful vine, by the way, with distinguished leaves more or less cut, like those of a Japanese anemone or maple or the human hand, and some are more deeply cut than others. Some are almost lacy. It looks delicate, and I thought it would be handsome in one part of the garden, so I let it grow from a bird-dropped seed.

But it quickly overwhelmed everything in its path, romped up a medium-large Norway maple, and killed a vigorous white wisteria — just smothered it. I never knew anything could smother a wisteria, but when I was away for a couple of months the dire deed was done.

In early fall great clusters of the berries, somewhat like those of the Virginia creeper, turn a gleaming blue with tiny black dots. Like other members of the family, the Boston ivy and so forth, it can be a plant of embarrassing vigor, and like some of us it gives little hint in its slender youth of the giant creature it becomes with age.

Many other of our native plants vary in agreeable ways. The wild yellow azalea, *Rhododendron austrinum,* can have rather thin strappy flowers or they can be full, and the color can vary from one plant to another. Good nurseries take care to propagate the best forms, and I always felt lucky in my Tennessee garden to have a really nice one, approaching orange and dazzling in bloom.

It is well known that roses sometimes sport; that is, genetic accidents may happen on some twig or other, changing the flower color, and these may be propagated from cuttings. One of the most beautiful "old" roses is 'Variegata di Bologna', a three-inch, globular, very double flower of white with dark purple-red stripes that turn to purple with age. It has the very strongest kind of scent and is wonderful except it blooms only in spring with me. But this year one flower appeared that was solid color, the color of the stripes. No doubt the striped form was a sport of some old dark red rose, and now the striped form was sporting back to the original color. Such things add interest to the garden, though they are of no practical importance.

A friend of mine, Roberta Case, sent me a root of a pink water lily she had found in some remote part of, I think, Michigan. She felt it was wild, not escaped from a garden or deliberately planted. It bloomed this past week and is a surprisingly beautiful pink flower, the outer petals intensifying almost to red near the heart of the bloom. The leaves are fully circular, like the wild *Nymphaea odorata,* and the new ones are rich red-bronze, turning to green with age. The flower suggests the garden variety 'Rose Arey', which I have never grown, but I suspect this one is different. Mrs. Case calls it 'Shupac Pink' for the lake where she found it. Whatever it is, it is one of the most beautiful of hardy water lilies, and shows the wisdom of keeping one's eyes open.

Working the Bugs Out

I HAVE TWO FRIENDS, both reasonably steady middle-aged men, who can be counted on to come screaming and roaring every spring when they see an aphid or a caterpillar. If they possessed nuclear arms and if somebody told them (and there is always some nitwit to tell them) that that would control aphids, they would have blown up the capital before now.

I have never comprehended this fascination with aphids or bugs in general and attribute it to some regrettable trauma in childhood, probably no longer treatable.

It's true that one of these men has a rose that is likely to put on a poor show because he cuts off flower buds every day to show people how the aphids have chewed off the ends of the buds. One of these years he will notice, I imagine, that that particular rose does not have pointed buds. They are truncated, as if the tips were chopped off. They also have a rosy and greenish tinge before they open. He attributes that to aphids too.

He has no intention of taking my advice to leave the fool rose strictly alone. Of course it's not going to bloom if he keeps cutting all the buds off to show the world what the awful aphids have done.

This year I think I have some leaf miners in the roses, and as far as I am concerned they are going to stay right where they are. If they become so serious that the rose is weakened, then the rose will have to recover by itself or else be pitched out. I am in some ways a rather natural man, and certainly I follow Nature in not coddling roses.

I do not spray anything, partly because I have noticed over the decades that the average gardener who does spray gets no results whatever from his efforts except to do in a certain number of innocent insects, though the plant shows no benefit whatever, and partly because life is too short to spend on trying to turn various poisons into flowers.

On rare occasions I have with regret squashed a tomato hornworm, a beautiful green and white and black beast, but in general the destruction of bugs does not interest me; they go their way and I go mine, except for basketball-size hornet's nests when they are near the ground and right next to a public sidewalk or (as once happened) fourteen inches from the outside water faucet. On those occasions, I hire somebody to get rid of them, however costly that is. One hornet sting below the eyebrow is enough for me.

A Little Work, a Lot of Glory

❋ SOME OF THE RICHEST effects in gardening come from flowers no larger than a quarter. Often I run into gardeners who have only a moderate passion for plants. They like things that more or less look after themselves, and I often wonder why they do not concentrate on just two or three fine spectacles in the year, and forget about beds that require continual weeding, and forget plants that may be delightful in themselves but that never make much impact even when in bloom.

At the moment, few things are as dazzling as the little-known rambler rose 'Polyantha Grandiflora', which despite its Latin name is a garden-variety plant first raised in France in the 1880s. It has glossy foliage and immense quantities of single white roses, about one and a half inches wide, borne in round clusters the size of large oranges.

The perfume is intense, with a musk sweetness. On a fence it would probably cover forty feet, and it is ideal for growing up such trees as a yew, an old apple, a pear, or perhaps a locust or sophora — something not too dense.

If you had a great plant of such a rose, its beauty would be magnified if the tough and easily grown clematis 'Etoile Violette' were planted to wander about through it.

Even more dazzling would be these two plants with another rose in front of or behind them, for instance 'Mrs. Flight', with clusters of small semidouble rose-colored blooms in fat clusters as large as small cantaloupes, and with the purple, nearly thornless rambler rose 'Violette' mingling with it.

These four plants alone, given their head to run up trees or hedgerows, would make a spring spectacle worth a detour to see. They all bloom only once a year, and only for two or three weeks in May. But once planted from small plants and given generous treatment (buckets of rotted manure and substantial waterings once a week the first year), they would within three years make large creatures. They would need no attention whatever in later years. They would hold their own against weeds (except bindweed, grape, or any other vine that kept all the sunlight off them) and would be a joy for years to come.

It is indeed a disadvantage that they bloom for so short a season, but I feel, when their brief season is done, that it has lasted long enough. Such roses have a way of hanging out from the tree and making a fountain downward, and unlike climbing hybrid tea roses, they are the last word in grace. And also unlike hybrid tea climbers (which are gorgeous, of course) these old ramblers are paved with flowers. The effect is more sumptuous than that of any other kind of rose, and they do not suffer from black spot (sometimes a bit of mildew, but no need to spray).

The purple 'Violette' is scentless, but the great white rambler can sometimes be smelled fifty feet off. I strongly commend such a planting to gardeners who simply do not have the time or the inclination to tend regular garden roses.

For an earlier display, few things equal daffodils in the grass. You would want hundreds or thousands of them. Not the magnificent modern daffodils of the show table — they do not have constitutions strong enough to survive in grass — but kinds suitable for naturalizing. There are plantings of daffodils that have been in place more than half a century without having been dug up, divided, and replanted.

The main thing is to let the leaves die down naturally, not mowing the grass till mid-June and again in the fall, to keep it from getting too dense.

A third project, almost as labor-free as the first two, is a large fish pool or pond, stocked with hardy water lilies and goldfish and a variety of interesting plants (arrowheads, yellow water irises, thalias, rushes, striped acorus) in and around the pool here and there.

Much of the charm of such a feature is its freedom from drought and disease. There is endless pleasure to be had from frogs and toads, from dragonflies and damselflies that come unbidden and make the long summer days vibrate with life. All kinds of birds visit the pool to drink, and as they come at different times of the day, there is always something to see.

All three of these projects could be managed with less labor than is needed to keep a small lawn cut, and I continually marvel that so few gardeners try such things.

Quite gorgeous effects come from broad plantings of daylilies and irises, but they require much more labor if a varied collection is attempted. They are splendid for intensively cultivated city gardens, but the things I speak of today are just the ticket for gardeners who are by nature lazy and who have rather a taste for glory.

getting there is not important; the wandering about in the wilderness is the whole point.

July

Gardening Is a Long Road

IT'S UNBELIEVABLE that cutworms chewed off every single one of the nasturtium seedlings at my place, about twenty-five of them, before they emerged, while another twenty-five seedlings at another garden have not been touched.

Man and boy, I have known cutworms for fifty years. I never bothered them, they never bothered me. If they chewed a tiny plant here and there, well, cutworms have a hard life and I don't begrudge them a sweet pea along the way. But 100 percent? Before I even saw the cotyledons above ground? I would have said the nasturtium seeds were bad, except that the twenty-five that are flourishing came from the same packets as the twenty-five that never showed above ground.

One morning I did see, right at soil level, the stump of the slaughtered plant. All the others were cut below the surface, showing no sign of varmint damage to the aboveground eye. At least now I know. I replanted the nasturtiums, all of which have emerged safely.

A beautiful wild plant, *Canna warscewiczii,* has plain green leaves with a wire rim of red and a few small scarlet flowers like the old Indian-shot cannas that grow wild around poor shacks in the country. For big, flashy flowers this wild canna is a poor choice, since it produces nothing like the great bouncing beauties of garden cannas.

But the way the leaves are disposed of on the stem, and the modeling of the leaf, is a revelation to anyone who has seen only garden varieties.

I got the seeds years ago from the Royal Horticultural Society and always saved a few seeds, as the roots are not hardy in my garden. But as it has been about three years since my last seeds were harvested, and as they have lain bare on a fireplace mantel (occasioning cries and quite narrow rescues from time to time) I was unsure they would still sprout.

I planted them in a fourteen-inch pot, soaking them for twenty-four hours first, and to my surprise and pleasure a good eleven of them sprouted within a week or so. The babies are reddish, and the tiny leaves strongly curved like seashells. I admire them daily. It is very like admiring a baby's ears or toenails, so impressive is the perfection of the miniature.

And no cutworms, heh-heh.

A gardening friend who is far gone in subtropical stuff gave me three superb roots of ginger lilies. I gave one away to a woman who lives in an apartment and who had bad luck with ginger lilies two years ago. The others I planted near a pool, and they have finally sprouted. I do not know what they will turn into, as the man grows several kinds and colors. I hope one of them is the commonest kind, the white *Hedychium coronarium,* which for years I grew in Tennessee beneath the outside water faucet in the dog's yard.

Another treasure is the kind of elephant ear they grow all over the place in Louisiana. Its curving leafstalks bear the leaf blade horizontally, not hanging down like elephant ears on the animal. I do not like the ones that hang down.

Anyway, Mr. Mann arrived from Tennessee with some roots of the kind I like, and I planted them in tubs weeks ago. We had much rain and cold overcast skies. I feared that they had rotted, though I dug about every few days to assure myself the roots were still firm. Finally one big green shoot has emerged, and surely all will now be well.

This same gentleman, knowing my fondness for the Southern smilax or Jackson vine, *Smilax smallii,* sent me fine tubers the size of potatoes over a period of years, but not one ever sprouted. Finally I broke down and bought one in a pot for a couple of dollars from a nursery, and now the vine grows gangbusters on my porch.

I was afraid the Louisiana elephant ears would turn out like the smilax, with the disadvantage that I have never been able to figure out the correct name of the kind I like and would not know where to buy one. So this belated sprouting is uncommonly welcome.

Sometimes along alleys or in cracks of stone curbing you see my favorite petunia, which must be close to the wild one from Mexico. Its rather small flowers are off-white or pale rose or lavender, fragrant at night, and steady-blooming from the end of May till mid-November. I dug up a few and put them in large pots devoted to sweet peas, night jasmine, and so on. The idea is for this half-weedy petunia to hang over the edge and add interest to the pot and to set off the flashy main occupant.

I think it will be far otherwise. The infant petunias, the minute they perceived they were in rich soil with daily watering, took off like eagles. They almost certainly intend to swamp the sweet peas. You cannot believe how quickly the petunias, from one scrawny stem three inches high, have developed numerous stems or branches, with leaves greatly increased in size and luxuriance.

Once an ambassador was here from a country that gets no sun or heat, and he went overboard on petunias. He wanted the kind with flowers like tissue-paper tennis balls. He had them all over the place. Every loud color he could find. Well, I went through that stage in 1933, when the big double sorts were rare. "The seed is far more costly than gold," my mentor said at the time. And a good bit less desirable, if I may say so.

Now my ambassador buddy from the far frozen north simply missed 1933, as you might say, and his arrested petunia development has not worked itself out even today, for he still fools around with them, though they protest the lack of sun and heat.

All gardeners are at different stages. They must be gone through. Sometimes the gardener is stopped at some stage and never gets past it. I am that way with members of the agave family. I doubt I shall ever get over them and their cousins the furcraeas and dasylirions.

But I am over the fat petunias. I have no truck with them. I hew to the elegant tough wild kind that is so sweet at night, that grows with such vigor and that retains such neatness all summer.

Gardening is a long road, with many detours and way stations, and here we all are at one point or another. It's not a question of superior or inferior taste, merely a question of which detour we are on at the moment. Getting there (as they say) is not important; the wandering about in the wilderness or in the olive groves or the bayous is the whole point.

Sunflowers and Memories

SUNFLOWER SEEDS please a lot of birds, notably cardinals, and we use 150 pounds a year in the bird feeders; therefore, like everybody else who carries on in this way, we have plenty of sunflower plants sprouting in the spring.

These are weedy, of course, with their big fuzzy, scratchy leaves, and do very little to enhance marble pavilions (if you happen to have such a thing — they also do not go very well with gilded statues of George Washington), but at my place, where they are by no means the only weeds, sunflowers are handsome enough.

Usually I weed them out in May, but this year I left one, which began to bloom early in July. I feel better every time I look at it. Some of the most beautiful of all garden prints in the past have been of sunflowers, and I suppose most gardeners know the Claude Monet pictures, too.

The sunflower is an American flower, of course. It would do quite well, as far as I am concerned, as the national flower, and while we think of it when we think of Kansas and similar outposts of the empire, it flourishes virtually everywhere, provided it receives sun and heat.

I have never been quite sure about the sunflower of William Blake's wonderful lyric "Ah, Sunflower," which is one of the extremely few successful poems of the language written in anapests.

Anapests are almost invariably a mistake. Which is no doubt why Blake was determined to show they can be dandy:

> Ah, sunflower, weary of time
> That countest the steps of the sun,
> Seeking after that sweet golden clime
> Where the traveller's journey is done;
> Where the youth pined away with desire,
> And the pale virgin shrouded in snow,
> Arise from their graves, and aspire
> Where my sunflower wishes to go.

He may not have been thinking of our American sunflower; other flowers share that common name. But the English have always loved our sunflower, and garden books of the last century commonly showed a neat young woman standing beside a sunflower that had reached sixteen feet beside her cottage.

To this day there are people who like to see how tall and how large they can get their sunflower to grow. They wish to possess the biggest aspidistra in the world, so to speak, and it is a harmless enough endeavor, though nothing to the purpose of fine gardening, as Francis Bacon would surely say if he were around to pontificate further.

There is no sweet scent to the sunflower. I always associate them with the scent of June bugs, which clustered thick on the plants I first knew. There was a railroad a few blocks from our house to which we kids were forbidden to go, since there was a hot tamale shop down there that (my Aunt Frances Bodley said) sold tamales positively fatal if eaten, unless one were Spanish or something. Besides, she said (and we had no idea how she knew) it was an utter den of utter iniquity and you would not believe the things that went on there.

Years later, with the boldness of a teenager, I surreptitiously went to the place and was terribly disappointed that the iniquity was pretty moderate, and consisted largely of paying for the tamales, which were excellent and not fatal thus far, and I am no longer a teenager.

Anyway, the train tracks were lined with sunflowers I remember as being 165 feet tall. Perhaps they were not quite that; a little boy on a daring errand of viewing the prohibited sunflowers by the prohibited train track near the prohibited tamale shack is not the most reliable of reporters.

Many a summer morning, however, I viewed them, with the tamale stand on the horizon, and therefore comprehended early on the paradox that high beauty and evil may coexist.

One year I grew some fancy sunflowers that were double, the size of melons, the flowers with petals like a shredded carnation. They came in both the usual yellow and in red. As with so many novelties, they seemed rather on the marvelous or gee-whiz side, but they lacked the style of the plain railroad-track sunflower and I never wished to grow them again.

Near us was a place called Ashlar Hall that I suppose startled people who were not expecting a Norman castle on the Tennessee-Mississippi border. The chatelaine was remarkable partly for jack-knives off the diving board at the age of eighty, and partly for a night-blooming cereus that required four men to lift when it came indoors in winter, and which on some nights had sixty-three blooms open at once.

But the great thing was that right in front of a massive limestone column was a single sunflower every year. It probably would not have been the choice of the architect, but we all admired it greatly in the fall, when little birds hung on, pecking out the seeds.

But even aside from the sunflower's role in art and in memory, it is a glorious, robust, dignified I-am-what-I-am sort of flower. Wherever there is full sun, and a gardener not too delicate and not too fancy, it should be found.

Stalks and Bonds

✿ JULY IS A GREAT TIME for lilies, though it is often too hot to admire them while the sun is out.

I see that one stalk of the white trumpet lily somewhat absurdly called 'Black Dragon' is eight feet tall with many flowers. I bought it decades ago when it was new and expensive, but now it is widely raised from seed, producing lilies quite similar to the original clone. Like other lilies it likes leaf mold and flawless drainage.

Another good and relatively easy lily is 'White Henryi', which has bowl-shaped flowers of white with a salmon or orange star in the center. It inherits much of its good, healthy disposition from its parent, the wild *Lilium henryi*. This year the bulb has produced six flower stalks five feet high or so. Unfortunately, like its wild parent, it needs to be staked or supported by shrubs.

Several years ago I received a pecan-sized lily bulb from a friend at the National Academy of Sciences, who in turn received it from a small chain of former owners. Thought to be a rarity, the parent of this lily, *L. myriophyllum superbum*, has virtually disappeared from gardens but was found at a botanical garden in Burma.

That flower was crossed with some tough yellow-trumpet Aurelian hybrid garden lilies, including 'African Queen'. When those seeds grew and flowered, the best one was crossed back to *myriophyllum superbum*, which is also known as *L. sulphureum*. So the second seedling generation bulbs are one part Aurelian hybrid and three parts *myriophyllum*.

The aim was to produce a yellow trumpet having the beauty of the wild parent found in Burma with the garden toughness of 'African Queen'.

The bulb I received was black, quite dry, and soft, so I had no real hope it would grow. But I planted it in pure humus in a steel tank two feet deep, and it grew, very weak at first, but after two years it has produced three flowers, a beautiful waxy yellow deeper than canary, with bronze flushes on the exterior.

I am no good at lilies and cannot evaluate this second-generation hybrid, but while it is beautiful it looks to me like a regular yellow-trumpet hybrid and not as magical as its fabled Burmese parent is said to be.

In any case I have selfed the three flowers, and if seeds result I'll turn them over to the academy, and possibly the genes of the Burmese parent will be useful to those who raise lilies better than I do.

Plants That Make Their Own Elbow Room

MOST GARDENERS have a bad habit of planting things too closely or (with potted plants) not shifting them to larger vessels as they grow. Which is why I admire agaves.

These "century plants" are native to our southwestern regions and Mexico. They do not stand freezing, or not much, and cannot be grown outdoors all year in most of America, but they do splendidly outdoors from the end of the lilac season till early November.

I have several, collected from the trash when owners did not want to bother with them further, and they now occupy twelve-inch pots. The thing that amuses me about them is that when the pots get too small, the agaves simply crack the pots apart. They remind me somewhat of terriers, who also believe in doing what they jolly well please and never mind the consequences.

I was surprised to see in Madagascar such a variety of our native agaves, especially a small one that when mature is only the size of a bushel basket, which has whitish margins to the leaves. When it flowers, the blooms produce thickened tissues like bulbs, with a tuft of leaves growing from them. The plant in bloom seems to be crowned with dozens of infant plants atop the twenty-foot flower stalk. These drop as the stem rots, and if they find good ground they grow along into new plants.

The century plant is so named because it was thought to bloom only after a hundred years. In fact, it blooms when it gets ready, which may be only several years. Then it dies, but usually there are offsets (gardeners call them pups), which soon grow vigorously, so that where there was one agave there may eventually be a clump of several.

Many succulent plants of this kind in the lily family are monocarpic; they flower and set fruit once, then die.

Another plant that takes things into its own hands when the gardener is backward about giving it more space is the water lily. These grand watery beasts should be repotted, or retubbed, every two or three years, but sometimes the lazy gardener neglects them. You will wonder how I know so much about lazy gardeners — a case of observation, merely.

Often water lilies are planted in good dirt (no sand, no leaf mold, no peat, but good heavy clay loam) in plastic tubs. These look imperishable, but after about three years the water lilies ram a hole through the side and escape. You can always tell when this happens, as the plant suddenly takes on new life and doubles or triples in size.

If water lilies are given a heavy wooden tub that they cannot split apart like plastic, they may require another year or two but then they climb out the top (by elongating the main tuber or by producing subsidiary buds on the tuber). They grow down to the bottom of the pool till the roots hit that nice gunk on the bottom, then they take off like the side-splitters.

The lotus — and this may be the place to say that the common Indian lotus with semidouble pink blooms is as beautiful as any flower can be, and more beautiful than some of the garden hybrids — is even less patient than water lilies. Its very first year, if it has good heavy soil and endless sunlight, the six-foot leafstalks eventually weaken and bend down into the water. They then thicken at the base, and the new tubers grow far beyond the original tub.

Once I had a circular pool ten feet across with a single lotus tuber planted in the center. It did seem to me the lotus was going mad so that soon the entire pool was thick with leaves, and the point of the pool was lost, as the water could not be seen.

Upon investigating, when somebody asked if I could spare a tuber, I found the entire bottom of the pool was solid with perhaps three hundred tubers the size of bananas, all strung together like great beads. I gave him a wheelbarrow full of tubers, which promptly filled up his shallow lake in the country.

Our wild native lotus, which is yellow, is equally vigorous, but most of the garden hybrids are not; they behave better, or at least more slowly, in the pool.

Even quite vigorous plants may suffer or even die out if competition is too great. My great clump of striped grass (*Miscanthus chinen-*

sis variegatus) used to reach ten feet, and the clump expanded reasonably with each passing year.

Then I planted a gray-leaf butterfly bush, or buddleia (named for a Mr. Buddle), about three feet away, and it died the second winter. *Buddleia crispa* is one of those plants that are perfectly hardy but manage to die every winter. So I replaced it with a garden variety, 'Ile de France'. Now the buddleia has shot up to ten feet, grievously shading the striped grass, which last year almost died out. I was sorry to see that it reached only knee height. This year I butchered the buddleia, and the striped grass responded somewhat, reaching four feet but still sulking. The only way I can restore it to its ten-foot glory will be to cut the buddleia to the ground and keep it to chest height, a difficult thing to do in our wonderful soil and climate.

Of course, sheer greed is the problem here. I like the vast silver fountain of the striped grass against a wooden wall painted black. On the other hand I also like all the butterflies and hummingbirds that come to the buddleia. As gardeners so often must do, I let the buddleia have its way till it almost kills the striped grass, then whack it back. In this way I manage to have neither plant in perfection, but I do manage to have both, where there is room for only one.

Often when people see such a thing they think the gardener does not know how big plants get. Ha. The gardener knows quite well, but is greedy and wants both. Greed in this case is not far from love, both of which exact a price in this world.

Every Garden Needs a Weed Patch

❀ THE FIRST WAVE of lightning bugs came at the end of June, and while we had a lone damselfly early in June, we have not had any dragonflies well into July. I've read that purple martins gorge on dragonflies, and therefore I do not regret the birds' refusal to nest in this garden. The dragonflies are far more valuable to me than the martins.

One of the important advantages of being American is that on summer nights the millions of insects start to sing. Are they late this year? Surely they used to begin their elegant chorus the first of July in the past, but not this year. Although it will be another twelve years before we have the great emergence of cicadas by the million, every year brings a few, and enough to contribute mightily to the morning and evening chorus. If gardeners stopped thinking of insects as enemies they would find some pleasure in them. Butterflies alone are reason to forget poison sprays. Here I have only silver-spotted skippers, various swallowtails, and white cabbage butterflies, or at least those are the ones I recognize and see often in summer.

Every garden should have a weed patch of nettles, dock, thistles, and milkweed for the benefit of these epicurean beasts, and even a quite small garden should have a buddleia, as no plant attracts them better. The lavender variety, 'Lochinch', is a good choice as it grows to only five or six feet, but if there is plenty of space, many other varieties in electric violet, mauve, rosy lavender, and white could be added. Cannas are said to be attractive to butterflies, and while I am only moderately fond of those plants, I hope butterflies will come to *Canna iridiflora*, a tall kind more tender than most. As far as that goes, I hope this canna will grow and bloom here. It is rare in gardens, and my plant is small, but hope springs eternal, or at least with surprising frequency in the gardener's heart.

Surrendering to the Ceiling Fan

❀ MID-JULY IS SUCH a voluptuous season in the garden that every gardener rejoices in it, even if the heat is insupportable between ten and six — at least the garden is splendid at five or six in the morning, which is when the gardener trots out to pick perhaps a dozen tomatoes from his three plants.

And as the sun weakens, he can admire once again his four-o'clocks, both the kind from Peru and the kind from our own American West, long white tubes that flare only half an inch wide.

The last of the *auratum* lilies are seen, and the trumpet vine (especially the garden variety called 'Madame Galen') is exotic, with its melon-sized clusters of apricot-orange trumpets twice as large as the wild native kind. And nothing is prettier than the double pink bouncing Bet, one of our prettiest weeds, and the pale yellow to white 'Italian White' sunflowers, and the green nodding bells of *Nicotiana langsdorffii,* which is by no means showy but is full of interest in a modest way and combines well with everything else.

Daylilies are good now, and of the 13,000 garden varieties (literally there are that many) surely the gardener can find a few that please him.

Already in bloom is the sky-blue *Salvia uliginosa,* and soon the huge white trumpets of the daturas (I have got over my passion for red and yellow ones) will make up for the passing of the great white *Magnolia grandiflora.*

Any day now the blue dawn flower will begin, that elegant perennial morning glory from South America, which ought not to be hardy but is.

There are endless things to do in the garden, for those who like labor, but the indolent gardener, like the no-account grasshopper in the fable, may take his ease and sing through the rest of the summer while the industrious ants among us do the right thing and sweat mightily.

There is one labor worth doing, and urgently needing to be done if one is new to the great garden irises of today, and that is to prepare a bed within the next few weeks so that it can settle before the iris rhizomes are planted toward the end of August.

I already have my irises, so I need do nothing except admire their foliage, still looking good. Next July I shall have to dig them up and divide them, but sufficient unto the day is the evil thereof. Let's not think of next year now.

You recall the account in the play where Falstaff dies and thinks of eternal things, but Mistress Tearsheet comforts him, saying surely there is no need to think of such things yet. We shall wait till cool weather to think of all the things left undone and still ahead of us to be done.

The iris bed, to add a word about it for those new to these gorgeous creatures, needs to be dug no more than a foot deep. A two-inch layer of fully rotted horse manure, and (for perfection's sake) a two-inch layer of good sharp sand, can well be incorporated in the digging, but no other fertilizer is necessary or desirable.

The iris roots can be planted anytime from now to mid-October, though I have found they do especially well if planted after August 20, when the worst of the heat is over (even if some of the hottest days occur in September, briefly).

The fleshy fat roots are covered with half an inch or an inch of soil, no more. They are given one good watering, and thereafter, in our nearly flawless climate, they take care of themselves for a year. It is only necessary to keep weeds out, and then in January to scratch or hoe over the frozen ground to get up any chickweed that may have got started in the winter.

Beginners with only a few irises may plant them as close as a foot apart, though in the long run, over the years, it works best to allow three feet between individual rhizomes, as they can then be left alone for three or even four years without the need to dig them up and divide the surplus plants that have come along. If planted as close as a foot, they will have to be divided within a year or two years at most, but the effect the first spring after planting is better if the plants are close together, even if it means more work in digging and dividing them sooner.

If irises are planted after mid-September they are less likely to bloom the following May, but irises planted in late August come along well and bloom as freely their first spring as those planted at the end of June.

The critical thing is sunlight — they need all the sun they can get, and they need good drainage, as they will rot if water stands on them.

On days when energy is high, I may spend as long as ten minutes pushing the young growth of moonflower vines toward their support (provided by fences or wires up a pole). Once they find something to twine around they are on their own, and the gardener need do nothing whatever except see to it they do not get dry. A bit of watering once a week — nothing more onerous than that is needed to produce their masses of scented, salver-shaped, pristine white blooms.

The gardener owes it to himself to spend much time beneath ceiling fans. It is bizarre and possibly immoral to get plumb tuckered out leaping here and there. In July it is the gardener's duty to drink iced tea or lemonade — why are people nowadays too lazy to squeeze lemons? That is a thing far more worth doing than bounding out in the heat of the day simply because some tiresome scold says you should do this and do that. Take my advice, tea and lemons.

Keeping Watch on the Water Lilies

IT'S MY OWN FAULT, of course, for being extremely fond of water lilies, so that now, it strikes me, an inordinate number of people ask me about them.

It ought to be said somewhere that no water lily is more beautiful than our native wild *Nymphaea odorata,* the scented white water lily found in ponds over most of the eastern United States. It is recognized by its circular (not horseshoe-shaped) leaves of fresh pea green.

It should always be grown in a tub, not in earth in the bottom of a pond, since it spreads with optimistic vigor and soon becomes an embarrassment in a natural pond. But when confined to a tub holding a cubic foot of earth or so, it behaves rather well.

Honesty compels me to say that no water lily I have ever grown behaves all that well. Even the least vigorous sorts, once they settle in for two or three years, start peering over the side of their tub and sending down roots into the mud or mulm at the bottom of the pool. The gardener is commonly surprised when he lifts the tub, or tries to, to discover that half the plant is over the side and rooted firmly on the mud bottom.

The very worst, in this respect, is the common pink lotus from India, *Nelumbo rosea.* It is sometimes said, possibly by people in harsh climates or by people who do not know what they are talking about, that if a lotus is given a circular tub its tuberous roots can go round and round contentedly for two or three years. Ha. No plant in the world is more beautiful in leaf and flower. But a sharp watch should be kept to ensure that the lotus stays within bounds.

I was rather pleased, and not much surprised, to notice at the Kenilworth Aquatic Gardens that the pink lotus there had traveled beneath a dirt road ten feet wide into a pond on the other side.

In the South, the native yellow lotus grows so densely at the edges of lakes that it's hard to get a rowboat to shore, and many a pond built for cattle has become solid with this lotus. All of which is splendid. But the gardener should not suppose he can simply plant a lotus tuber and forget it and that it will still make a lovely clump three years later. No. It will have covered the entire pool.

Against a wall facing north I have a small horse trough of galvanized steel four feet long and twenty or thirty inches wide and two feet deep. It is additionally shaded (not only by the wall) on the east by a hydrangea I am fond of — with leaves blotched white — and on the west by a grape, 'Monticello', which gets so little sun I fear it will never fruit.

I do not expect miracles. And water lilies, of all plants, adore the full sun without any shade at all at any time of the day. But of course they make do with less than perfect conditions. Do not we all.

But my problem in this small tank was to grow something green. I could hardly expect a water lily to flourish or even endure in so sunless a spot. And the trough is too small for a nuphar, or spatterdock, that admirable genus of a dozen or so species, which grows in running (as well as stagnant) water and which endures colder temperatures in the water than any of our garden water lilies. It has, moreover, beautiful leaves that rise a few inches out of the water. The blooms are like little doorknobs, clear rich yellow, but no larger than a quarter or, at best, a silver dollar. Compared to the showy water lilies of gardens, they are pretty plain, but their foliage is even waxier and more leathery than that of regular water lilies, so the nuphar does have its uses.

But it likes to grow very large, making great rafts of leaves in cold rivers of the Ozarks, for instance, and my shady horse trough is much too small for it to show its beauty, so I ruled out the nuphar.

I did pop in a tub of the yellow water lily 'Chromatella', an old Marliac variety that came out about 1888. It is exquisite in its beauty, and I really prefer it to some other yellows I have grown that are theoretically showier. It is well known that 'Chromatella' endures more shade than most other hardy water lilies, but even so it should have about four hours of direct sun each day if it is to flower.

Imagine my pleasure to see 'Chromatella' flowering in the almost sunless horse trough. Not as large, not as richly colored as it should be, but living and blooming half-heartedly with hardly any sun at all.

If I had endless space I'd grow every water lily in cultivation — there are several hundred kinds — and I think they must all be beautiful; certainly, all the ones I know about are handsome. And I shall not weary you with discussing varieties again. But I see new gardeners err in one thing when they are planting water lilies in their pools. Sometimes they think they will do the water lilies a favor and give them really splendid soil to grow in, with plenty of leaf mold, a bit of peat moss, plenty of rotted manure, and so on.

This is a mistake. Manure, while splendid if it is cow manure and very well rotted, can add so much organic life to the pool that for two years (and maybe forever, for all I know) the water will have a distinctly green cast.

Goldfish think it is glorious, and they grow with astounding speed in such rich green water (assuming each little goldfish has five square feet or so of water surface — otherwise they will not only not grow fast but will speedily die, since the minute organisms that turn the water green also use up a lot of oxygen ordinarily available in the water for the fish).

But the gardener does not have that sparkling black crystal look, with a golden cast, that he likes to see in his garden pool.

In choosing earth for the tubs in which water lilies grow, therefore, I would avoid all natural manures. Once the water lily is established, in a few months, and when it seems to be slowing down a bit in its growth, a handful of 5-10-5 chemical fertilizer may be rammed down into the mud of the tub without taking it up out of the water. You want to be excessively careful, however, not to use any of those fertilizers that have weed-killers in them, because they will kill the water lily with great promptness.

Actually, in the garden pool the great problem is keeping the water lilies from covering the entire surface, not making them grow. You want, after all, open space to reflect the sky, not a solid mat of green water lily leaves.

Ordinary garden dirt does quite well. I have read that water lily roots do not readily penetrate clay, but that is not my experience. I have always found that the more tenacious and sticky the soil, the better the water lilies like it. They do not yearn for woods soil or leaf mold. They abhor peat. They should not be given sand, which has no nourishment in it; in a mere cubic foot of soil you do not want to short-change the water lily by giving it sand.

Dirt that seems to you right for growing good roses, peonies, oaks, will do nicely. And try to give each water lily plant a good cubic foot of earth to grow in. That is more, by the way, than the gardener thinks it is. Some gardeners are not very cubic minded, of course, and say to themselves, "Oh, I imagine this bucket is about a cubic foot," when it is not. Gardeners who do not think in cubic feet should think in bushels. Give each water lily a bushel of earth.

And always full sun. Unless, of course, the pool is partly shaded, in which case do as well as you can and hope for the best. And be grateful.

Would anyone willingly live where the watermelon, the sweet corn, the blue water lily will not?

August

A Gardener's Weather Wonderland

❀ BEFORE A HURRICANE hits and knocks us off the map, I should remind gardeners that the climate of the capital is one of the most favorable in the world, and rightly is the envy of all.

A trifle warm in summer, yes, but would anyone willingly live where the watermelon, the sweet corn, the blue water lily, will not? The winter is a bit colder than we like, but if it were any warmer the gardener would have no daffodils, tulips, peonies, or lilacs. Below Washington those flowers are iffy.

We have the best of both worlds, and it is unspeakably wrong to whine at the weather gods.

Gardeners commonly say of the English climate that you can grow anything there. It is easy, they say, to garden there. On the contrary, it is astonishing they even attempt a garden there, so sunless are their skies. You expect to wait decades for a young magnolia to bloom. You wait a century for a yellow poplar to make a respectable specimen. You forget about ever eating a good tomato again, and settle for those little reddish golf balls that pass for tomatoes there. Forget peaches and melons, crape myrtles and dogwoods.

And in Britain, even when the garden does finally come into its beauty it is commonly too cold, too windy, or too cloudy to enjoy it.

King Charles I used to say England had the best climate, as one could be outdoors more days of the year than in any other climate he knew. He was executed, though not for his odd views on climate, and to put an end to all foolish envy of the dreadful climate of the British Isles I ask a simple question: Why does an Englishman, the instant he can manage it, get out of England to seek the sun in Spain or Italy or America or, for that matter, Egypt or India?

True, he usually longs to return home, but that is merely conditioning, as cats try to return home if you don't butter their paws, even though the new home is superior to the old. No doubt somebody buttered our forefathers' paws when they came from Britain a few centuries ago, as I never heard of any of us going back to England or Scotland to live.

No country is more civilized than England, except maybe Denmark or Holland or Sweden, and all those nations have much to be proud of. But a beautiful climate for gardening is not one of them.

Having said this, I think it outrageous that the crape myrtles are more than a month late coming into full bloom here this year. This has been an inadequate and un-American summer, vastly too cool and overcast. The skies must endure our rebuke and mend their ways. We do not need another summer like this.

I hear reports, indeed complaints, that a "golden ladybug" has been eating holes in leaves of moonflower vines and certain morning glories. I have sought them in vain on my plants, though I had them for several years about thirty years ago. A bug person identified them for me as cantharid beetles, a family best known, or most infamously known, for a product that stimulates desire by irritating various sensitive body tissues. Even in my most experimental phases I had sense enough not to try anything so dangerous, but I did admire the metallic gold of these beetles. As in the Poe story "The Gold Bug," they indeed seemed to be made of hammered twenty-four-karat gold. In death the gold disappears completely, so it does no good to keep a few to admire indoors in winter. As for controlling them, I never tried to, and only hope they will return someday. The damage they do is moderate, and hardly to be weighed against the pleasure of finding them dazzling on a leaf.

With me their favorite plant was *Ipomoea acuminata,* the blue dawn flower from South America, which used to be called *Pharbitis learii* and used to adorn the roof of every proper greenhouse and conservatory. My two plants have not bloomed this year; neither have they attracted any gold bugs. Nothing is ever perfect in the garden, just as nothing is ever fully disastrous.

I found a dwarf (seven-foot) bamboo from Japan, *Shibataea kumasasa,* listed at the fancy price of $100 at a Louisiana nursery. This bamboo, which accepts trimming into a hedge of waist or chest height, is supposed to be hardy only south of Norfolk, but I have grown it for decades in our climatic zone here. In rare zero winters it turns brown, but usually it remains deep vibrant green all year. In winter the leaves sometimes develop a withered margin, and this is attractive.

Although always considered a clumping bamboo, not a running bamboo, it does stretch out a bit, and a plant will gradually spread to twenty feet after fifteen years. Thus I have often asked friendly gardeners if they would not like a start of it. They usually say no, as most gardeners are afflicted by a phobia of bamboos in general.

This year on two occasions when I asked the question, I got out the catalogue listing the plant at $100, on pretext of double-checking the name, and let the visiting friend see it. In both cases I found homes for this bamboo, which I will gladly share next May with anyone as long as the supply holds out. Free, of course.

The Wings of August

WE ARE UP TO OUR EARS with birds in the garden, most of them welcome, and after fifteen years of not venturing inside our fence the crows have concluded it's now safe. I liked them better when they sat on neighbors' roofs and just looked.

Both mockingbirds and catbirds can be seen at almost any minute of the day, and cardinals dependably show up early and late in the day. Carolina wrens chatter rebukes almost any place I walk, as they have young in nests, and a tubular bird of brilliant canary with black wings has turned up, along with nuthatches, tufted titmice, purple finches, and all those less distinctive birds I call sparrows — incorrectly, in many cases.

Street pigeons have mercifully vanished, through no action on my part, and sea gulls do not come closer than four blocks away. They would make short work of the goldfish in the tanks, no doubt, so I hope they never discover them.

Hummingbirds are to be seen almost every day, though not in the numbers I'd like, and I've seen them investigating the late-blooming daylilies and roses as well as their more usual buddleias, trumpet vines, and monardas.

The squirrels built a summer nest in the crotch of an old maple and then abandoned it, as I could have told them they would. It was about twenty feet off the ground, but there were no leafy branches near it, just the massive bare wood of the trunk and main limbs. So after all that work, they moved far up in the maple, maybe forty or fifty feet, and now seem satisfied. We hope this year to keep them from moving into the attic in December.

Earlier in the summer we were sorry to see a number of Japanese beetles in the garden, as we never see them at all as a rule, but they did no damage and have now disappeared. We have no starlings this summer, which is quite unusual, and thus far only one blue jay — the last three years we have had none, though formerly they were as thick as mockingbirds.

What with viburnums, mulberries, plenty of grapes, and other oddments in the neighborhood, they seem to be eating pretty well. They like the combination of open space and thick hedgerow-type growth, and they like the constant supply of water provided by the main fish pool, which I try to keep brimming.

I miss the big flickers and pileated woodpeckers that used to visit us, but several smaller woodpeckers have favored us with daily visits ever since we put out the suet feeders.

Among dragonflies we have the usual heavy representation of the bright blue ones and occasional massive bronze ones, and a few damselflies, also blue. We have no lizards or toads, which I greatly miss, and more than anything I wish we had some of those black skinks with yellow stripes and metallic blue tails. If there is any place to buy some I'd like to know it. I have ideal conditions for them: plenty of sun-warmed masonry, billions of leafy twigs, and undisturbed compost in which the young could grow. (The young are much larger than the adults and look very different.)

Well. The moonflower vine began to bloom the last day of July, and a double orange-apricot Chinese hibiscus (which comes in for winter) only started flowering early in August. Our very beautiful native *Hibiscus coccineus* has not bloomed at all, because it has not grown very much, because it is in too dry a place. This lovely shrub, which dies to the ground every winter, has deeply divided leaves like a hand and crimson flowers. I know many gardeners like those big mallows, but I don't, and do not know why they are commonly grown while the far more elegant wild hibiscus is overlooked. Probably it's because nurseries sell the one and not the other.

Another native flower virtually impossible to find is the great coneflower, *Rudbeckia maxima*. It is madly different from any of the rudbeckias like black-eyed Susans and 'Goldsturm'. The one I speak of grows from Missouri to Texas and has oval leaves that lie on the ground in a big basal clump, and they are glaucous like cabbage leaves. The flowers are clear yellow with a three- or four-inch brown cone in the center, much longer than other rudbeckias. Why it is rare I cannot say, since it is handsomer than all the others. Its somewhat leaning flower stems (though they never blow over or fall down) grow to seven feet.

I spent a day off watering my rambler roses, the ones nobody grows (to speak of) such as 'Aglaia' and 'Violette', and I admit they are rather a nuisance, as the new growth has to be tied to the arches on which they grow, and it's more work than most gardeners think is justified for roses that bloom only a couple of weeks a year. And many are scentless. But I think all gardeners grow a few things that other gardeners wonder at.

It amazes me that so few gardeners grow crape myrtles. I don't myself, but never mind that, I can't grow everything in my small city garden. But for most gardeners the crape myrtles make far more sense than, say, rambler roses. There are new kinds raised by the National Arboretum, and those might be investigated. They do not get mildew in September. But the kinds that have always been grown do not get enough mildew to bother me.

Apart from the usual watermelon-red kind, crape myrtles come in white, clear pink, lavender, and purple, as well as red in other flavors than watermelon. They are perfect for small paved gardens, having beautiful flowers for two months or so, plus colored fall leaves, plus mottled bark that looks fine in winter. In 1933 I had my picture in the paper in the town I grew up in, with the mayor standing beside me. We looked equally stupid, as I recall, but the point was that I was planting a crape myrtle that had been proclaimed the official tree of the city. It does seem so long ago, and I often wonder if those crape myrtles I planted as a kid are still in that garden.

Things Are Doing Better Than Expected

❀ HOW BLOWS the citron grove? It's the question Adam was always asking in Eden, and while a small town garden is not a citron grove, necessarily, the gardener still trots out to see how things are coming on.

The waxy white stephanotis buds all fell off during the rainy spell, I see, and several other small disappointments commonly await the gardener upon his return after a few days away from the grove.

Other things are doing better than expected, including the cannas, crinums, black-leaved sweet potato, and, notably, the orostachys. The name means "mountain spike," and the various kinds of orostachys come from Japan and China. They are biennial, books say, but behave as perennials, coming up every spring with new vigor.

If you never saw *O. aggregata,* the species I have, you would suppose it is a variety of sempervivum, or hen-and-chickens, as we call them. There are slight differences, and the orostachys is a little fleshier in the leaf. When it feels like it, it sends up a little column of flowers four or five inches high, not at all showy and suggesting the flowers of a sedum.

It creeps along the earth, the rosettes remaining only an inch or two in height, but these little rosettes of leaves are densely packed. As the name suggests, there is soon quite an aggregation of them.

I had a tall terra-cotta pot of amphora shape until it was knocked over and lost the top twenty inches. An uncommon little pink that had formed the crowning tuft of this pot lay belly up on the ground. But how well it all turned out. The pink was stuck back in the now much lower pot and an orostachys was planted beside it. The orostachys has carried on like the most fertile of rabbits, and the pink with its blue-green grassy leaves makes a pleasant contrast with the fat rosettes. It is a plant of no particular consequence, but it is typical of hundreds of plants that make no great show but that are full of interest to the gardener.

Most gardeners are familiar with the catbrier or greenbrier, a climbing, spiny, leathery-leaved weed that you see supporting itself on the underbrush at the edge of woodlands.

Far handsomer is the Jackson vine, *Smilax smallii,* which romps all over the lower South but not as far north as Washington. It is doubtfully hardy north of Norfolk, books say, but I have known it to flourish in our Zone 7 for decades without protection. Its long pointed evergreen leaves and (eventually) black berries festoon all manner of important occasions, from dinners to weddings, in the South.

Many times I have tried to transplant it, as its massive fleshy tubers the size of pokeweed tubers suggest it is easy to establish. But the tubers never sprouted for me, and finally I got a small plant from a nursery. The first year it sent up a spindly stem to three or four feet, and this was accidentally cut down (not by me, you may be sure) and through my anguish I said, oh, no harm done. The next year it shot up to ten feet on a trellis at the front porch, and this year it clearly wished to turn the corner, so I gave it a catenary swag of insulated telephone cable.

The best thing about the phone company is that linemen are

forever leaving piles of cable in the alley when they finish a job, and every gardener worthy of the name collects it, stores it somewhere, and gets it out for many a good use, such as tying in branches of the yew and box so snow does not break them, and for luring climbing roses back to their supports when they start wandering off to find more light.

And this year I used the cable to haul a blue-leaved cunninghamia tree upright against a fence. For several years it had crept along the ground.

So now the smilax is growing along its cable and looking quite handsome. Ordinary wire, rope, and twine are all too flimsy to support the smilax once it gathers strength.

The Topic Is Tropicals

❀ SOMETIMES TRUMPET VINES fail to flower well in their early years, but if the vine is healthy looking there is no need to fidget. If the vine gets half a day's sun and ordinary soil it will flourish, often more enthusiastically than the gardener has counted on.

There are good reasons that any particular plant does not flower, but if the gardener has provided the right conditions for its growth he has done all that is necessary. It often happens that if a plant is growing too lushly because of heavy watering and fertilizing, it will not flower until growth slows down. This is apparent in climbing roses, wisterias, and various other vigorous climbers.

It is not generally known that the tropical moonflower vine produces fertile seed that can be gathered early in November, stored dry, and planted indoors in pots in April, to be set outdoors in permanent positions in mid-May.

Although the fleshy roots do not survive the winters at my place, in some years new plants appear as late as June from seed shed the fall before. Sprouting so late, however, the plants may grow to only ten or fifteen feet, so the better plan is to collect the seed and start it indoors the following spring.

A plant rarely grown in the capital is *Clerodendrum bungei* from China and northern India. It is surprisingly hardy despite its tropical look, though its woody stems are usually killed to the ground in winter. New growth from below ground appears in spring and reaches five feet or so by late summer.

Flowers come in dome-shaped clusters about six inches across, and the hundreds of small tubular blooms are rose red to purplish red. It is a highly fragrant creature, and it blooms from time to time during the long warm-weather season.

In winter it is a good idea to give it a heavy mulch; in spring a good dressing of rotted manure, along with heavy watering, will ensure vigorous growth and flowering. While this plant prefers full sun, it performs well in spotty shade, and I have seen it doing well against a north-facing wall here.

Most other members of the family are strictly tropical. They can be grown in pots or tubs outdoors in summer but should be kept indoors at about sixty degrees during winter.

I hope I am not mentioning too many subtropical plants that may seem new and strange to town gardeners. I know how discouraging it is to read of plants not often seen at garden shops. There was a time, however, that such ordinary occupants of gardens as gladioluses, cannas, caladiums, dahlias, and so forth were rare and thought to be exotic indeed.

Even in an unusually cool summer we still are blessed with sun and temperatures that suit many tender plants. Consider petunias, zinnias, and marigolds — mainstays of many gardens, yet all of them from hotter climates. And even those plants that must come in for the winter are often easily grown in tubs, which have the advantage of being easily kept free of weeds.

In small town gardens where priority usually is given to paving or decks for sitting outdoors, I sometimes marvel that the small space available for plants is given to marigolds — not that there is anything wrong with them, but after the first million days of their flowering, looking the same week after week, they become tiresome. Often it would please the gardener more if the space were given to subtropical vines (moonflowers, certain morning glories, coral vines, purple-leaved sweet potatoes, solanums with white or blue potato-type flowers, and so on).

And among big perennials or shrubs for tubs there are rich things among oleanders, night jasmines, and other cestrums, ginger lilies (some of which are surprisingly hardy in the open garden over winter), tuberoses, crinums, lemon verbenas, and endless other treasures from Mexico, Africa, Australia, and warm parts of Asia.

My gardening friend Mr. W. has only a somewhat shaded strip at the side of his row house, but it is fully stocked with angel's-trumpets, passionflowers, bananas, strange cannas, and much else. I have never quite had the courage to ask what his small house is like in winter when half of equatorial Africa moves in. A little advance planning helps.

Pleasures of Plants by the Pool

NEIGHBORS SAY they have sometimes heard frogs jump into my fish pool, and one neighbor said he saw a frog, but then he likes to say encouraging things. So today nothing refreshed me more than to hear a truly solid *plosh,* which could have been made only by a frog of some stature.

My viewing chair for the pool is not well placed, as a horse trough with tomato plants sits between chair and pool. The tomatoes now rise ten feet in the air, and the only view is through the gnarled old tomato stems.

The brick walk at this point is twenty feet from the kitchen door, and as I look toward the house from the viewing chair I see several treasures now at their best, starting with the great trumpet vine 'Madame Galen' on the house wall. As this wall faces north, and as the trumpet vine is a sun-loving Southern belle to end all Southern belles, it took five or six years to convince the vine that it really did wish to flower on this bleak wall after all.

Now it rises two full stories, the dark green foliage spangled all over with clusters of apricot-orange bloom. I have noticed more than once that I often succeed with handsome weeds and get fine effects from them.

One of the good-looking things between chair and house is a clump of hyacinth bean, the result of sowing five bean seeds in a metal cylinder that held ice cream in its palmy days. Something I admired (and learned) in tiny gardens around shacks in the cotton fields of my youth was that a surprising assortment of beautiful plants can be grown in small containers, provided they are watered every day or every other day.

A tub of water holds some agreeable things, the tropical *Pachira aquatica,* which in a better world than this (or a milder climate) becomes a small tree with pincushion flowers of red and white, pollinated by bats. Also here is a fine specimen of the wild Japanese iris in its variegated form, grown for its leaves, though its violet flowers are welcome when they come in June.

The white form of cleome, one of our prettiest native weeds, grows surprisingly well in a couple of six-inch pots, and the shape of its flowers contrasts well with everything else.

There is a fine plant of Simon's bamboo, which is simply sitting there until I decide on a permanent site for it. There is a large tub of common lavender, with the violet-blue scaevola growing over the edge, and now in bloom in a pot too small for it is a rare form of summer hyacinth, which looks very much like the common *Galtonia candicans,* and a rare salvia (the name written down somewhere) that does not care to bloom.

A large pot of vivid magenta-pink dianthus is in flower, and next to it a pot of three-foot-high *Thunbergia battiscombei,* with small tuba-shaped blooms of vivid purple.

The last flower is out on a seedling daylily, a cross of 'Green Glitter' and 'Bitsy', and the clump has produced flowers since June 15. Nearer the chair is a spike of the pink crinum 'Cecil Houdyshel'.

Boccaccio wrote a fine story, "The Pot of Basil," which inspired me to plant five seeds in each of two pots. They are enough to produce the sweet basil scent and lush leaves. The Italian story is a good gory account of what happened to the head of an adulterous lover, but they had larger pots than I do.

On one side is a horse trough full of miniature water lilies and a couple of tall *Thalia dealbata.* This pool, seven feet in diameter, is home to some fat but vigorous fantail goldfish.

New buds have appeared on the white angel's-trumpet, *Brugmansia candida.*

There is a pot of wax plant, one of the *Hoya* genus, now in flower and trained to its three-foot stake. The flowers hang down in the leaves and thus are not showy, but I admire them every day.

I have overlooked a few odds and ends, but the point is that rich colors and fine shapes can be grown in a very small space by anyone. No skill is required, but steadiness is. Watering must be done every day, but it doesn't take long and is a pleasanter responsibility than mortals commonly take on.

Awaiting the Last Blaze of Summer

THE LONG HOT DAYS with thunder are soon coming to an end. Already the signs of approaching fall may be seen — the first flowers on the wild white almond-scented clematis, a brilliant red leaf here and there on the dogwood, swamp maple, and sourgum trees.

But early September may yet show us some of the hottest days of the year, all the more wonderful for being the last true burst of summer.

Some days I have sat in the open summerhouse, roofed with a grapevine now in fruit and good for the birds (the variety is 'Monticello'), and from there I can see the length of the garden. It is much overgrown, though the rambler roses on arches over the brick walk were pruned in good time, and a horrendous job it was.

On a blazing afternoon the grape makes it possible to sit outdoors. All over the temperate world people have hit on this same device of a small paved place to sit, shaded by vines.

If you take the train from Washington up the East Coast, you often see modest row houses that have no real gardens, but often a square of concrete (originally sacred to trash cans) graced with a couple of chairs, and some poles holding up an improvised arbor for grapes.

And recently, in *Life in Alanya,* Washingtonians George and Cecilia McGhee describe their life in a Turkish village, with details of the local *chardaks,* which are simply raised platforms like our summerhouses, only open on all sides and shaded by a grape or other leafy screen from the sun. At night, even on the hottest nights, such places are good for sleeping. That is one reason they are raised, to keep rats and snakes off. The McGhees say the Turks have inordinate fears of these creatures, but then they are none too popular in Washington either.

From my grapy sanctuary I can view the sea of green, too shapeless now to suit me, but at least abounding with life. Water lilies and reeds and the beautiful *Acorus calamus* in the form with pale yellow striped leaves are doing well in the pool, and the agaves in big pots have borne the cooler-than-usual summer with solid grace, though other heat-lovers such as daturas and brugmansias have sulked.

My enthusiastic admiration today centers on a quite tender canna, *C. iridiflora,* the iris-flowered canna of Peru. It is said to tolerate far less cold than ordinary garden cannas, which is probably why you never see it in gardens here. A quite small plant with two leaves arrived in late May, and I suspected it would take two or three years to raise it to flowering size. On the contrary, it has grown to shoulder height and is now flowering.

An established plant reaches ten feet or so, with leaves three feet long and a foot wide. Flowers are borne on curving drooping stems at the top, and the rich coral-rose flowers, smaller than those of garden cannas, hang down. They resemble individual florets of a gladiolus, except for seeming to hang upside down.

Three friends from England saw the plant and were only routinely polite. No fits. I have often thought the most intense pleasures of a garden are reserved for rather odd people.

I will not try to mulch this plant's rhizome to preserve it outdoors over winter (a process that works well with many marginally hardy plants) but will dig it up in November, dry it off for a couple of days, cut the stem down to within four inches of the root, and store it in dry wood chips in a chilly room, examining it from time to time to make sure the fat root is not shriveling. If it is, I'll sprinkle a bit of water on it, shade it off, and put it back in the chips; I will start it off in a pot in April, to be set in open ground in mid-May.

The most elegant gardens always retain a certain earthiness.

September

Bulb Essentials

MOST GARDENS, however small, have wasted space that is ideal for such small beasts as snowdrops and crocuses. Everybody loves the crocus, and fortunately a good many varieties are now easily found at stores that sell bulbs, though I can remember when such beauties as the *Crocus chrysanthus* hybrids ('Ladykiller', 'Snow Bunting', and so on) were virtually unavailable to casual gardeners.

And no garden should be without snowdrops. The old common kind, *Galanthus nivalis,* with nodding white bells, is the best, once you get over the lust for rare forms of this elegant flower that brightens February.

These, like other small bulbs planted now and in October, are best put in as soon as available, except for the various small wild tulips (*Tulipa chrysantha, clusiana,* and such), which go in during the first three weeks of November.

It is well to plant daffodils now, though like most gardeners I have planted them long after Christmas — why not do things at the proper time? Of daffodils there is not much to say beyond urging you to try smallish ones of the *jonquilla* and *cyclamineus* sections of the family. Few daffodils have given me more pleasure or such abundant bloom as, for example, 'Quail'.

There are, however, few daffodils that are ugly, though many are a bit gross. To begin with there is nothing better than the yellow large-cup 'Carlton', a sensation a few decades ago and still unsurpassed for planting in quantity. It was bred by the late P. D. Williams, who in some ways was the greatest breeder of sound garden-variety bulbs.

Just now the hyacinth bean, with tropical, lush, coarse foliage touched with purple and great upstanding racemes of purple-and-white bean flowers, is at its best. Peter Hattch at Monticello told me this simple annual vine (maybe grown by Jefferson, maybe not) causes more comment than any other flower there.

The tropical water lilies from seed have produced only one flower, a nice if ordinary pink, and the great angel's-trumpets (*Brugmansia*), which I counted upon to be proud sentinels near a small raised pool, have barely grown at all, let alone bloomed.

The tea roses ('Madame Berkeley', 'G. Nabonnand', and others) have done poorly, and my favorite old 'Princesse de Sagan', a fragrant red China tea, was accidentally destroyed in a sweeping cleanup.

Several times I have attempted to grow the lovely weed common toadflax without success. I know why. It loves the edges of gravel and the edges of sidewalks beneath chain-link fences set up by construction companies. It also likes relatively barren hillsides, all very different from my heavy, rich soil in which things are jammed together.

I see it in waste places in Boston, along with bouncing Bet, milkweed, small wild asters, lilies of the valley (now with red seed capsules), mugworts, and a few other common but lovely old stagers, now banished from elegant gardens (except the most elegant, which always retain a certain earthiness).

God willing and the creek don't rise, I shall improvise a small four-sided box with an old glass sash to accommodate my three Parma violets. Otherwise, I might bring the fourteen-inch pot indoors to a cold bedroom by a south window, and hope the violets bloom there.

These violets are not much seen now, and they are only favorites of the last century, so they have none of the immemorial associations of ancient flowers. But they are fragrant, and suitable for Victorian matrons, of which this capital still has the type if not the originals.

A flower that might not immediately strike a beginning gardener, but which every old codger knows is indispensable, is the Japanese anemone, with stems waist-high bearing clusters of single, silver-dollar-sized white flowers with yellow stamens embossing the center. The single white is best. For some reason I had to plant it several times before I had a good clump going. It blooms in September and October. Even in a crowded town garden, room must be found for it.

The Beauty of Vines and Weeds

❀ A FRIEND OF MINE, perhaps less precise and gifted in her analysis of weeds than in her judgment for matters of great importance to the American state, recently heard of that terrible affliction of mine, the bindweed, and (not finding any in her own garden) ripped out the first vigorous clematis vine she saw.

I wish, first of all, that I could see no difference between a clematis and a bindweed. How agreeable it would then be to say my garden is quite overrun with clematis that I really cannot control — they just take over everything.

And I am glad, second of all, that she has had this tragedy. Yes, glad. There is a strain of viciousness and envy in all gardeners I have known, usually brought on by failing with some plant to which one has given the greatest attention, while one's friend (who has given it no care at all) has it running all over the place. The lady in question used to lose no opportunity of exclaiming how the Japanese anemones were running her out of house and home, knowing quite well I had planted them repeatedly without the least success.

Now, of course (for pigheaded stubbornness often pays off in the garden), my Japanese anemones are as good as anybody's, but for years I had trouble, and for years my friend gloated mercilessly. And now that she has yanked out a perfectly good clematis, we see that justice from the heavens may sometimes catch up, heh-heh.

But although I have suffered heavy blows this summer from the bindweed and other disappointments too numerous to bore you with, I looked out my bedroom window this morning with joy. Just below the sill was the finial of the simple garden house, the pyramidal trellis roof of which is covered with climbers.

The grape 'Monticello' has been heavy with purple clusters, but it soon gives way on the garden-house roof to *Clematis paniculata*, now densely studded with its flower buds and inch-wide white starry flowers scented like almonds, and tangled with it is that good pinkish honeysuckle, *Lonicera heckrottii,* which has been a mass of flower ever since April. No honeysuckle I know of even touches it.

Just beyond in my line of vision, so that the water seems to touch the clematis and grape and honeysuckle, though in fact it is fifteen feet distant from them, is the pool with pink, yellow, and blue water lilies. I promise to say nothing more of them, since I have praised them recently.

The rest of the garden is a living mess.

Except the northwestern corner of the house, now decked with the great flower clusters of the hybrid trumpet vine 'Madame Galen'. It really is a sheet of flower, and I am all the prouder of it since it gets little sun, and everybody knows the trumpet vines need full sun. Still, this is the place I wanted it to be, and I hoped it would think it was in a hedgerow in Tennessee, where one often sees trumpet vines that get fairly little sun yet bloom contentedly.

It has surpassed my hopes, though it took a few years longer than I thought it should, and now hummingbirds hover about it and land on its branches so you can get a really good look at them.

I say nothing, of course, of the clouds of sparrows that have taken to roosting in the trumpet vine at night, nor of the complete assortment of bees, wasps, hornets, that come to explore it. Like everything else, if high perfection is the goal, you have to see it on the right day and at the right time, and ignore other factors like the sparrows at dusk.

Where I walk (or run) every day to catch my bus, I tread on many plants of the beautiful chicory, one of the loveliest of meadow flowers. Here it is mowed down every couple of months, so it grows only a few inches high. Its sky-blue daisies are handsomer than plenty of plants I have grown with some effort.

What would be prettier than a bed of this wild chicory, interspersed here and there with nasturtiums or scarlet hardy carnations and an occasional phlox or some bouncing Bet (another beautiful weed) or some sadly mauve cosmos and a few white cleomes (a grand weed that, if whacked back in late June, will branch low and bloom until November).

Such a thing would certainly be handsomer than a solid planting of begonias or geraniums or marigolds, and the only work would be to keep the bindweed out, and in the spring it could be pretty solid with daffodils and tulips that would make way, as they fade, for these lovely summer weeds.

Another tremendous pleasure of the late summer is the sound of the cicadas and crickets and other melodious creatures whose names I do not know. They have been chorusing for some weeks now, and nothing in the whole year is more worth waiting for. But all too soon, as fall comes, the chorus will diminish day by day, then suddenly stop, and only the crickets will sing for a few days longer.

In downtown Washington you do not get this beautiful chorus, but a few blocks out from the most congested traffic you do. I was outraged to read that some idiot government bureaucrat was busy telling people how to kill the cicadas this year, but then there are probably tax-paid bureaucrats in Italy giving directions for how you can get that cruddy paint off Leonardo's walls.

Recently, taking the terrier out to Great Falls to gaze at the ducks and slop around in the canal, I saw the first metallic blue-tailed skink I have seen in the capital, though I am not sure whether it was a three-lined or a five-lined kind. I wish I knew how to establish a colony of these skinks in my garden.

There was a vigorous colony in my former garden that had lived there more than sixty years. For some decades they lived under an old wisteria and later, when it was taken out, they moved a hundred feet to the east to a compost heap, after which it was of course forbidden to use that compost or dig around in it.

These are things you can't just go to the store and buy, and I hope those who have skinks are aware of their privilege and admire them fully throughout the warm season, when those brilliant lizards bask on sunny walls and pavements, a splendid sight denied to most of us.

Trailing Away from Summer

THE WINDUP OF SUMMER is a glorious season in the garden, though a bit too like the end of a holiday to suit most gardeners.

Although I feel like a squirrel that must race about storing nuts, there is time to revel in the soft light and fine skies and to gather in the bounteous harvest, such as it is, heh-heh. And before any gardener works himself into a fit about the oncoming winter, he should remember winter is a bugbear word to terrify children, when in reality the most beautiful skies of the year come in winter.

Thus braced, we see what is retrievable of our early spring dreams.

Two vines, much neglected by gardeners, are in beauty now. *Parthenocissus henryana* is a cousin of the Virginia creeper and the Boston ivy. It has divided leaves like a hand, somewhat velvety gray-green-bronze on top and reddish beneath. The top surface has a white line running the length of each leaflet, and the new growth is soft salmon-colored.

It is far less vigorous than its relatives and has a limp, confident, laid-back luxuriant look, and about November it all turns red like its cousins, enlivened to the end with the pale stripes. I find it beautiful on a wood fence or a wall, and if I had a mature hawthorn I would let it clamber up that and hang down in swags.

Tiresome circumstances have kept me in Boston for a few weeks, and it's odd the plants you suddenly miss sharply when you're away for a spell.

In Boston the common wall vine is the Boston ivy, which is good for converting any deadly expanse of poorly made concrete walls into a luxuriant mat of green, turning red in fall, so it has claims to usefulness and even beauty. But its greatest beauty is seen when it is let loose on a half-dead Norway maple, clinging upward for thirty feet and hanging down in rich folds, and the same is true of the Virginia creeper.

The effectiveness of these last two vines may be seen in Paris, where they are planted at the top of the retaining wall of the island on which the great church of Notre-Dame stands. They hang in clotted rich ropes to the Seine and provide a perfect example of a common plant displayed to strut its richest beauty.

But of all these cousin vines, the most beautiful is the species *henryana,* which is said to be hardy only in Zone 8, but which I have long grown in Zone 7 and have known to take subzero temperatures without protest.

Another vine that seems more beautiful to me than to some other gardeners is *Kadsura japonica,* hardy to Washington and probably to Philadelphia, New York, and coastal Connecticut with a bit of shelter.

It has leathery magnolia-like leaves (being of that family) but only four or five inches long, sometimes slightly toothed, sometimes smooth, and of a rich bright green. The vine twines up a pole or sapling, and mine mingles on one side of an arch with an allegedly superduper form of the European honeysuckle, which looks like the usual yellow-madder European honeysuckle to me, for all its fancy added-on names.

When the kadsura blooms, fingernail-size white saucer flowers appear in axils of the leaves. Some authorities call them tiny, but they are visible enough, waxy enough, and sufficiently magnolia-like to enchant any steady gardener who has not fallen too far under the spell of fourteen-inch dahlias.

For all its white flowers, it is called the scarlet kadsura, presumably for its fall fruits, which look like tiny magnolia cones with scarlet seeds. Or, I often suspect, for its red stems when young (they turn gray with age, as who does not) or the salmon-red new growth, waxy but translucent, a distinct minor delight all spring and summer.

Though it is said to grow to fifty feet in Japan, I had it for years on an ugly hog-wire fence, where it shingled down like so many overlapping rich tiles, studded with white in late spring and red fruit in fall, interwoven here and there with the amber translucent twining new shoots.

A beautiful plant indeed and easily grown by any fool, but maybe too well designed and too elegant for those whose idea of a garden is a fifty-foot drift of black-eyed Susans or a whole hillside of forsythia (one of the asinine features of the Dumbarton Oaks garden, which illustrates what a garden designer falls into when she runs out of taste, brains, style, and sympathy with plants. Hence it is widely admired by some architects).

Now, now, must not be beastly to such admirers of the Dumbarton forsythia mess. They, too, have dogs that love them and most had mothers. I fear that absence from my own garden (the water lilies from seed are just blooming, and I won't see them or the great blue Brazilian morning glories or the third brave spike of the iris-flowered canna from Peru) — even this brief absence sets up a longing that too easily turns to ill temper.

Bless 'em all is the way to go. Though sometimes I think that when a competent designer plants a whole hillside with forsythia it's like turning a temple into a den of thieves, and a couple of runs of the bulldozer would restore the order and delicacy appropriate to a Washington hillside.

When you're away from your garden, it may be therapeutic to summon up some images you hate, to keep the longing for the beautiful capital under control.

Of Mice and Specimens

THROUGH THE KINDNESS of the director and the curator of woody plants, Dr. Stephen Spongberg, I had a beautiful morning at the Arnold Arboretum in Jamaica Plain, Boston, one of the world's great treasure houses of living trees hardy in northern temperate climates.

Already I had viewed some of the great sights of Boston, among which I rank highly the mice that live on the sunken tracks of the Park Street subway station. Between train visits these mice, which strike me as uncommonly small (and I see that people waiting for trains feed them wholesome bread crusts), dash on the black stones, perhaps old coke, between the rails. They bounce about in seeming frolic on the stones, but for extended journeys of ten feet or more they race down the flanges of the steel that serve as expressways. When they get vibrations of approaching trains, they race for the safety of their homes within cracks of the wall beneath the passenger platform.

At the great arboretum they have no mice, or none on display, but there are even greater sights for the gardener.

The paper-bark maple, *Acer griseum*, one of Arnold's many introductions from China, may be seen in a specimen with a trunk considerably thicker than a telephone pole, its exfoliating bark brilliant and tawny orange in the gray light of a rainy day. This tree, now very fashionable in gardens, is usually seen in young and therefore small specimens that give little hint of the tree's ultimate maturity and beauty.

I was drenched walking half an hour to reach the proper gate where Dr. Spongberg met me in a car, where in no time I was dry. We drove for two hours, hopping out at breaks in the weather to see splendid beeches as large and fine as those famous ones at Newport and Monticello.

Our superb native sour gum, *Nyssa sylvatica*, is unrivaled in fall, coloring from crimson to scarlet with a touch of orange. It had not yet turned color, but one branch of the equivalent gum from China was dazzling orange. I was told it was equally brilliant as our native kind.

As all gardeners know, there are Asian parallels to many of our best-loved American plants, including the yellow poplar, dozens of maples, oaks, fringe trees, dogwoods, elms, and so on.

The arboretum was established a century ago, but it required years for plans to be worked out, land acquired, seeds sprouted, and cuttings rooted, and only in our century has the original work come to maturity. Of course you see many young trees that will replace veterans in decades to come.

September is not a great month for flowering trees, but certain kinds, such as sophoras, are at their best, whether in flower or fruit, and a stunning specimen of the golden-rain tree (*Koelreuteria*) was at peak bloom. It is a late-flowering clone of the usual summer-blooming kind and is called 'September'.

Less flashy, but perhaps even more beautiful, is the tree named for Benjamin Franklin, *Franklinia alatamaha,* with white blooms that suggest both magnolias and camellias. The arboretum specimens, along with those of John Bartram's garden at Philadelphia (dating from the eighteenth century), are the handsomest I have seen. In favorable falls, the gold-stamened white flowers are still fresh as the leaves turn crimson in October.

Charles Sargent (for whom the famous old red camellia 'Professor Sargent' is named, by the way) was director here for fifty-four years until his death in 1927, and he virtually single-handedly made the place what it is today. But other men, such as E. H. Wilson, have added many superb plants. He risked his life more than once on his various exploration trips (hence his nickname of "Chinese"), and he introduced many plants of great garden merit, including azaleas, lilies, viburnums, roses, barberries, and much else.

A tree I have never admired much, but that some gardeners virtually worship, is the dove tree, *Davidia involucrata,* which is adorned with great white bracts hanging like so many snowy handkerchiefs waving in the wind. There were a few late blooms and many nutlike seeds.

Unfortunately, Wilson's roses collected in far western China are not maintained at the arboretum, their first home in the West. There are tremendous climbers of the musk or *Synstylae* section of the rose family that have a particular beauty not found in ordinary climbing roses, which, of course, are themselves glorious.

Within, I trust, the limits of politeness, I expressed dismay that the originals were no longer grown and the hope of all steady rose-lovers that the entire collection of Wilson's roses will be replanted eventually.

After a glorious morning Dr. Spongberg drove me to the subway and I returned to Beacon Hill, where I am staying for a few weeks. My head full of wonders, I did not pause to view my friends the mice at Park Street.

Houseplants and Other Migrants

BRINGING THE BABIES in for the winter is a chore gardeners think they will escape by not having houseplants to begin with, but it rarely is so simple a choice.

I have wound up with various houseplants over the years, mostly orphans dumped in alleys. I did buy for a dollar a dracaena eighteen years ago and don't ask me why. It was about four inches high. Now, though I have always confined it in a pot too small, it is eight feet with several nodding stems, and it has to spend winters in the living room in a spot with quite poor light. There it languishes and loses most of its leaves by spring, but revives when taken outside in May.

Sometimes I wonder if it finds life worth living, but it gets lugged in and out faithfully. I once knew a night-blooming cereus (an epi-phyllum) that was ninety-five years old and had 160 flowers open at once, if my memory is correct; certainly there were more than I ever saw or heard of on such a plant. It occupied a huge wooden tub with metal eyes through which iron pipes could be run. By holding the ends of the pipes, four men could manage, barely, to get it in and out as the seasons progressed.

The owner, who was given the plant (already an old one) as a wedding present, eventually became quite an old woman. For years she would invite the neighborhood to come see it on nights when masses of flowers opened. There would be ice cream and punch.

After her death the great plant was left out through a sharp freeze and that was that.

My wife keeps African violets in an east window in a bedroom. Someone recently gave her two fine young plants, and she said how nice that was, as her old ones had gotten ratty and worn out. Then she checked them in their summer quarters outdoors and behold, they were in fine fettle and blooming their heads off.

It is in such ways that the gardener winds up with houseplants, though he never intended to.

It is usually early November before I get them all in. Ideally, they should come indoors in September. If left out till nights are cold, they often sulk and drop leaves when brought indoors. All the same, it's November before I get them in.

Another pleasant chore I sometimes postpone, sometimes not getting around to it at all, is protecting outdoor plants that are more or less hardy but that benefit from more shelter than they get in the open garden.

After heroic efforts through some years I finally got a rooted cutting of the red tea rose 'Princesse de Sagan'. Nobody much would want it today, and I want it because it was one of the first tea roses I ever grew.

Just here I should say that tea roses are a class of roses, mostly pink or yellowish blends, that were parents of today's hybrid teas. The teas as a group have weak necks, so the blooms nod, and they are not very hardy to cold, though usually hardy enough in Zone 7 if given shelter from winter wind.

So this rose with me is now about a foot high. I will give it a virtual wall of evergreen branches, taking care it still gets light, and will mulch the ground around it with four inches of wood chips. That way it should go through the winter perfectly, and in a year or two it will be six feet high and loaded with flowers. Teas are not much bothered with black spot, and they are free in bloom sometimes up to mid-December.

Another thing I treasure is the noisette rose 'Jaune Desprez', which was bred in France about 1830. It climbs and makes a huge plant with stems two inches in diameter in two years. I think it is fully hardy here, but I always feel nervous about it. Early in December I give it a few bushels of cut branches, and sometimes after Christmas I lean a whole Christmas tree or two against it.

Two hardy palms also benefit from similar protection. Last year I did nothing, and the growing point of the Korean fan palm, *Trachycarpus fortunei*, turned to mush. Luckily, new leaves came out in spring, but this fall I shall be more careful with it and protect it.

I am quite proud of another palm, said to be even hardier, *Rhapidophyllum hystrix*, though as I have never done more than dig a great hole and plant it, there is no reason to be proud. There is also a quite beautiful evergreen vine, *Smilax smallii*, that undoubtedly benefits from winter protection when young (mine has grown only about four feet high), and the same is true of *Kadsura japonica*, a relative of the magnolias and a vine of modest beauty. I have had a well-established plant pull through twelve degrees below zero, but my present plant has been there only a year. A thick mulch of dry oak leaves should take care of it.

A Life's Garden, in Full Sum

❀ THOSE FEW SMALL low-lying clouds of white that you see a hundred feet down the garden walk are the hybrid musk rose 'Moonlight', which is not as fragrant as books say it is and not fully hardy, either, but I cannot think of a white rose more constant.

Twice I have lost it over the winter, which seems odd, as no rose seems to have, on the surface, a steadier disposition. It is not grand enough to claim a delicate constitution. It is, moreover, one of those roses that "grows all over itself" and makes a thick mound of branches and flowers. It is as tough as a blackberry, then all of a sudden one winter it dies outright.

Last spring a storm whipped into the metal arch over the walkway that this rose occupies, having been planted on both sides of the arch.

The weight of the rose branches bore down the whole construction, yielding one fine mess so that not even the terrier could pass.

In time it was cleared away and new growth sprang up from the old crown. I decided to saw most of the rose away, leaving two strong uptight stems that could serve as "trunks" for new little rose trees. Instead of an arch, in other words, there would be two little trees.

Unfortunately this simple sawing and staking never got done, so now there is a tangle of 'Moonlight' on both sides of the walk. Over the summer it has grown vigorously. It is in mortal combat with *Clerodendrum bungei* as well.

By next year the tangle will be even more formidable, and the tough yellow shrub rose 'Agnes' will enter the fray. There will be a week or so when the whole pile comes into glory, but sooner or later some grim hard work will have to be done to sort it all out.

In the meantime the white rose bursts into bloom every month or so, producing yard-long stems with dozens of roses not much larger than silver dollars. On certain days and in certain lights it can be beautiful even now.

Sometimes in great gardens I have seen rich tangles of flower that every visitor must admire. How farsighted, we all say, to have planned years ahead, with such care and such unerring taste, this picture of rose and clerodendrum, with the soft intrusion of pale yellow ('Agnes', you recall) to one side.

But the gnarled old gardener knows exactly how the picture was produced. The white rose and its steel support collapsed in a storm, and the gardener dawdled and time passed and behold — the rich new tangle never intended. Nevertheless, there it is.

Sometimes a whole section of the garden has to be cast anew. It may be easier to forget the little footpath and let the rose (hauled to one side after the storm) dictate the shape of that side of the walk. Easier than endless sawing and bleeding (where vigorous roses collapse there will be blood before things are set right), so that instead of the rich, neat arch of roses you now have mounds of roses with clerodendrum bursting through. And the yellow 'Agnes' taking advantage of some new open space has of course moved in to occupy what it can.

A garden ultimately, and sometimes with surprising speed, becomes the sum of decisions made after a spring storm has wrecked the original plan.

That is why a garden loses its character soon after the original gardener no longer tends it. A different intellect, a different judgment, takes over, and even though the same plants are still there, a different look is soon produced.

Some of the best (and worst, too, of course) effects are the direct result of coping with wreckage.

When I see 'Moonlight' down the walk, I see all the years behind it, all the different shapes it has occupied, all the winters to which it has reacted so differently and all the pretty stages it has gone through. I also see again those years when wild honeysuckle got into its crown of thorny stems, and the year the mockingbird nest was accidentally pruned out, and the time poison ivy got a start and had to be wrenched out blister by blister, as you might say.

All this and much more comes to mind when the gardener sees his 'Moonlight'. And this not his favorite rose by any means. What must his thoughts be when he deals with a plant he loves more and has lived with longer?

The point attempted here is this: a casual visitor sees one thing in the little clouds of white down the walk, but the gardener perceives much more. Not only does he see the same little puffs of white, but also he sees the streaming sweat of those times when honeysuckle and poison ivy had to be grubbed out. Not only the small dappled picture of this Labor Day but the garden over time, over years, and in spring storms and summer droughts.

It is not the little scene immediately before us, but the rich, complex, and often painful scenes accumulated years before that make gardening such a passion with some people.

What you and I see, glancing down the walk, is not necessarily the thing most worth seeing and most worth comprehending. The gardener sees something more, and it is what he sees that is important for him, at least, to understand, to acknowledge, and to give thanks for.

Friends at Season's End

🌸 THE BLUE DAWN FLOWER, *Ipomoea acuminata,* is finally in bloom, and so gracious are its three-inch salvers deeper than sky blue that I cannot complain, though I like it to begin in June, not September. As my plant was new this spring it got started late, and I hope next year will find it blooming right through the summer.

It comes from subtropical South America and thus endures some cold; I have grown it outdoors with only the shelter of a wall and a little mulch to tide it safely over a Zone 7 winter.

The flowers are borne in small clusters on six-inch stems, and while you would say they are the purest of blue, they in fact have much red in them, and this gives the color a somewhat electric quality such as you see in some gentians.

There is no need to think of September as the trash bin of the year, with just scraps of leftover things in the garden, because many things are only coming to perfection at the end of summer — a soft and gleaming season that reminds me of a long-eared hound with his yearly bath, sweet like a hay field.

I grow the dawn flower on the shelter built over the figure of a bronze beast from Bangkok, a perhaps foolish structure in which a pagoda roof of copper is held up by four-by-four wooden posts sheathed in copper. I built it myself, and sometimes marvel how I got it all up without any assistance.

Anyway, the vine grows up a post, mounts the curved roof, and gathers itself into a sort of ball or nest on the steel spindle that supports a weather vane. You have seen *Clematis jackmanii* growing this way, a tangle at the top of almost bare stems.

Other glorious vines flower now, along with this morning glory, which by the way is rather similar to the often seen 'Heavenly Blue', but which I think is even more beautiful and exciting.

The wild Japanese clematis with white stars only an inch wide, but perfumed with almond and displayed by the thousand, is also at its best now. It is often seen growing along alleys, but it is a flower of unsurpassed refinement. It is impossible to think how it might be improved. In addition to its flawless beauty, it is disease-free and bug-free, and it grows with all the vigor of a weed. I have seen an old maple, the trunk covered with ivy, and the ivy brightened by tufts of this clematis infiltrating it.

It is equally handsome growing up an old fruit tree, from which it hangs down in swags and garlands. It is beautiful also on any fence, transforming chain-link ugliness into a wall of flowery mist.

It can even be pruned. Sometimes I take hedge shears to it in summer, as late as mid-July, so the resulting growth flowers in October and November. I have even seen it clipped into a tiny hedge a foot high supported by those arched wire edgings sometimes seen around beds of annuals.

In all ways it is not only a perfect flower but a companionable one. Anything you want to do with it seems to suit it, and I can only stand amazed when I hear it dismissed as a common thing.

Equally robust and vigorous is the silver lace vine, which will cover a garage or a fence with an uncountable number of silvery white spikes of tiny flower. It can be grown as a vine to flower all summer, or it can be clipped and trimmed to force it into bloom only in the fall. It will grow right up a tree to thirty feet or so.

One of the most remarkable of all garden colors is the soft orange of the hybrid trumpet vine 'Madame Galen'. It is not quite orange, not quite apricot. It has a rosy tint to its trumpets, and it is always a soft and even coloring. Sometimes our native trumpet vine is harsh in coloring and, even worse than that, is often muddy.

Still another glory is the white potato vine, *Solanum jasminoides*. It has fat, starry flowers no larger than the wild clematis, but with a yellow button in the center. In full bloom it will make the gardener seeing it the first time contemplate theft or mayhem, whatever is necessary to acquire so showy and spring-fresh a plant.

What a garden could be fashioned of these vines alone. Not one of them is tricky to grow. Each one rejoices in our warm summers, endures our droughts and our downpours. All are healthy and madly vigorous. None needs coddling or prayerful watches. Why are they not seen in more gardens? I think it comes of not thinking ahead to plant them in spring, because the gardener then has his head full of daffodils and is giving no thought to the autumn equinox.

Two common weeds, the white boneset, like a too-vigorous ageratum, and the blush-pink bouncing Bet, with her soft fugitive fragrance, consort well with these vines. They are all virtual weeds, yet nothing I know of is lovelier in late summer. And all so healthy, so unstoppable.

Arches of Triumph

YOU HAVE PROBABLY SEEN those arches of tubular steel designed to span garden walks. They are usually covered with some kind of green permanent coating, and your imagination almost certainly runs to splendor, but let me suggest restraint.

No sooner did I acquire some arches than I planted them with some of my favorite roses, things like 'Mrs. F. W. Flight', 'Blairi No. 2', and other ramblers of pink and white that bloom only in May but then dazzle the eye.

If you do as I did, you will soon find yourself with arches groaning beneath a load of branches too heavy to bear. One good storm and they may topple over or be torn apart.

But (a gardener will argue) they grow old ramblers that way in the great public gardens of Paris. So they do. Only the walks are ten or fifteen feet wide, not the puny little paths we have in town gardens. And their arches are of heavier iron. In Paris they let the roses finish flowering, then lay the whole plant on the ground, loosening it from the arch. All the old growth (that is, the long canes that have borne flowers) are cut away at ground level. A few soft new shoots are retained, shoots that have never flowered and that are still in rampant growth.

These new shoots are laboriously tied in to the iron supports. The arches look naked. The effect is gawky until the next spring, when the arches are miraculously smothered with flowers.

The amount of labor required to tend to these roses is breathtaking. You really need a team, and a team that does not count hours or scratches.

If roses are attempted on these rather lightweight arches, such bushes as 'Mutabilis' are better than the old rambler. 'Mutabilis' is a China bush rose that turns itself into a sort of climber when given support. Its five-petaled flowers of buff and carmine (not scented) are glorious when viewed at a distance along a walkway, and the plant is in steady bloom from May to Thanksgiving in Zone 7 gardens here.

But I have been thinking how pleasant tomato arches can be. I have some 'Early Girl' plants that easily clothe such an arch to the top, bearing plenty of fruit from the end of June till late October. Each of my plants has already borne twenty pounds, and the developing green tomatoes in clusters are almost as attractive as the red fruit. Yes, of course, you have to stand on a ladder to get the ones that are high up.

I mention tomatoes as vines for arches chiefly to remind us that favorite plants can be grown in novel ways, providing amusement to gardeners, most of whom are as simple-minded as I am and as readily amused.

On the front porch or stoop a three-year-old plant of Jackson vine or smilax (*Smilax smallii*) has worked itself into a royal tangle, and I have spent some time untangling it and coaxing it to grow among a swag supported by the porch columns.

A certain amount of pruning has to be done, and at first the long shoots have to be tied to the curving cable with tarred twine (plain string, if it comes to that), but soon the thin, wiry tendrils will hold the vine to its support even in a hurricane.

The almost black green of its glossy leaves is so beautiful, especially in winter, that it is worth a little trouble. It is (or will be) especially handsome in late April when the pink *Clematis vedrariensis* (also called *spooneri rosea*) displays its thousands of blooms. You think the smilax is in flower. Unfortunately, just as I finally got the garland into handsome shape, looking rather monumental between the columns, a particular squirrel chewed great handfuls of the clematis and lugged them off for its summer nest in the high trees.

Squirrels are blamed for many crimes they are not responsible for, but in this case honesty compels me to say it was the squirrels done it. I saw them.

Another two years, however, and the garland of dark green and rosy pink will be back and will be (I trust) greatly admired.

Sooner or later some of our fine projects work out as dreamed. Then we are rightly smug. These little triumphs do not occur with deadening monotony, however.

One with Staying Power

NOTHING IN THE GARDEN earns its keep better than the sedum 'Autumn Joy', which has been in bud and bloom for two months now and will remain handsome for two months more.

Growing to a foot or two in height, it has glaucous leaves that are beautiful and substantial in themselves, from the time they begin to grow in early spring until winter finally claims them. But the main glory of the beast is its flowers, which appear as green-domed clusters late in July and grow larger, to the size of half a cantaloupe, in September.

At first they are glaucous green, then greenish white, then the half-domes are suffused with rose, then bronze and bronze-red. Eventually they darken, wither, and die, but only after having given week upon week of beauty. Sometimes you see those low wooden planting boxes that hold only four to six inches of soil, and they do perfectly well for an early spring display of pansies, but for year-long interest nothing is better than this sedum. It is easily propagated by pinching off two-inch cuttings and just sticking them in the dirt, for within a year they form a nice new clump. No disease or bug bothers it, but perhaps the most wonderful aspect of the sedum's garden usefulness is its facility for blending with all other plants.

I have a box of it overhung with trailers of the purple-and-white hyacinth bean, the flowers followed by red-purple pods, and as weeks go by the sedum forms a companion for the bean to flop on. Again, it consorts well with the brilliant yellow-green foliage of sweet basil, or virtually anything else.

Sometimes the gardener has a row of pots holding oddments of things that make no show in themselves but are good to have all the same. There may be, for instance, a few pots of lavender or thunbergia or night jasmine, or an infant furcraea, or young seedlings of Japanese irises, or a mature clump of the striped-leaf form of that wild iris. There may be anything and everything, and nothing is better than this sedum for giving a certain weight and dignity to a miscellany of pots.

In brief, 'Autumn Joy' is one of the few plants I would call indispensable.

I have already said something of the many uses of the wild white Japanese clematis, now blooming in gardens and alleys through the capital, but I should add another use — as ground cover. When this beautiful pest-free vine starts growth in the spring, it sends out long stems that latch on to any upright support they can find. But it may also be grown flat on the ground, as if it were ivy, where it will make a blanket of white for several weeks around Labor Day, into October.

Another beauty of the season is the silver lace vine (*Polygonum aubertii*), with spikes of off-white flowers. Gardeners sometimes rightly fear it, as it can romp up any young tree and smother it, and I have more than once cut it out as too vigorous and weedy for a town garden.

But it is too healthy and determined to be defeated by ordinary methods of slaughter. It comes back. I find that it can safely be allowed to grow over and among other things, like climbing roses, for example, provided the gardener stands at the ready with the hedge shears. You allow strands of the vine to grow and to flower mightily in October, then you cut it to the ground over winter. In this way you get its flowers without having it swamp everything within twenty feet.

This year the birds are eating the dogwood fruit before it turns crimson, and I am sure that is a bad omen. But then gardeners think most things are bad omens, and usually are right.

Just move it in early in October and out again at the end of April.

October

Autumn Tasks and Master Plans

FOR A MAN who dislikes houseplants (though if there were no outdoor place to putter about I would like them fine), it is odd that you can't get through the living room without being stabbed by a large agave and cannot sit quietly in the dining room without a seven-foot rubber tree leering down.

I expect every gardener to bring his houseplants in instantly. No excuses. Do it.

How often I have pointed out the importance of tying up Irish yews and other narrow vertical conifers because we get frightful snows here, damp and heavy ones, and when these are followed by wind the result is awful. The branches splay out and the whole tree is bent toward the ground. Simple folk imagine that when the snow melts the yew will resume its original upright posture. It is far otherwise.

Somehow I failed to do this the year before last, and my three narrow tall yews were ruined. Once the damage was done I got out there and tried tying them back into shape, and whacked off some big branches to coax them straight once more. If you will now tie the side branches in toward the trunk and maybe even sink a tremendous steel pipe behind them as a stake, you may avoid my woe. It will not do you much good to tend to all this after the yews are ruined.

Usually, when certain wild clematis finish blooming and are laden with clouds of feathery seeds, I leave them on until late February because the birds like to eat them. This year they cleaned all the seeds off by mid-October, and there is no reason not to tidy (whack back) the plants now. If not now, when?

But always I have tried not to ruin anybody's Sunday by listing endless chores ("Now is the time to mulch the entire garden with a six-inch layer of lark feathers") and do not now intend to start making myself miserable, either. But it does seem to me unfair that literally hundreds of necessary operations have been delayed at my place this year.

Before the great heat struck this past summer — and how glorious those weeks were — I dug up a congested patch of the old white trumpet daffodil 'Cantatrice' as the first step in digging up a lot of other daffodils that had been down (I blush, but I tell the truth) five to seven years.

This was part of a master plan to revamp the old plantings, dig new sites for a few hundred bulbs in May and replant in September. I wrote at the time of the proper way to prepare daffodil beds, so that when planting time came in October (though I prefer September, and have on occasion had to settle for February) everything would be ready and it would be sheer pleasure to dig little holes and set the bulbs in. Possibly my devotion to helping others delayed the master plan at my place. The bulbs, most of them, were not dug and dried, and the new planting stations are still a nagging dream.

The gardener who followed my good advice last spring will now be glad he did, of course.

Over the years I have learned that one way to revive a nearly dead plant with thorns or prickles is to plant it right by a main walk. Nine times out of ten it will start to flourish like a bay tree and will be a royal nuisance to anybody using the walk.

A ruthless friend of mine pitched out a beautiful plant of *Osman-thus* 'Gulftide' several years ago, and I rescued it because I didn't like seeing a perfectly good shrub sitting on the terrace with its roots in the sun, waiting for the trash men to pick it up in a week or so.

It sulked for a year or two but now has started to grow madly, especially on the side nearest the walk up to the front door. It does no good to prune it back because "strength follows the knife," as they say: the new growth is denser and more vigorous where you have pruned.

You might ask why any gardener would plant a spiny-leaved sweet olive right by a walk in constant use. Well, we do that because we don't think it's going to live. This year it began to flower in mid-October. I shall never cut it down now. The best hope is to get it tall enough that one walks beneath it, as an arch, and this may be inconvenient for four or five years.

Before I learned the hard way, I had trouble wintering fuchsias in the house. I kept them too dry. They certainly do not want to be kept wet, but they should be watered perhaps every ten days or so and kept in a cool room. If there is a room of the house in which the heat is kept turned off, this does well. So does an enclosed back porch. It is best not to trim the plants back until you see signs of swelling buds in March, then you cut back to five inches from the soil, give more water and more light, and put them outdoors at the end of April. If you keep them utterly dry (a thing that sometimes works with geraniums) they will be dead as doornails by January.

I hesitate to mention the following, since many houses are occupied not merely by the ardent gardener but by others who may be fussy beyond belief. But I now believe the best and safest way to winter tropical water lilies in the house (they will not stand the seven inches of ice that forms on our pools here) is to lift them with as much dirt around the roots as will fit into a large laundry tub or other vessel that holds water without leaking.

The leaves are cut off except for four or five small ones at the center, and the whole clump is set in the tub and covered with six inches of water. It should have as much light as possible, yet in many places there are objections to siting the vessels in front of windows facing south. Often one has to settle for a rather dimly lit basement. Sometimes, if there happens to be a twenty-gallon aquarium, the plant and its dirt may be set there and kept in a cool bedroom.

Ideally, one gives the old plant (which will just sit there marking time and not doing any growing to speak of) some heat, seventy-five to eighty degrees, in February, and full light from March on, and the whole thing is set back out in the pool on June 10.

Where conditions are not ideal, the leaves will die off entirely, but if handled as I describe, the large old tuber often survives and may be planted in the pool in June, even without any leaves. Given a decent summer, it will be in flower by the end of July and will of course continue to bloom until October 15, when the operation is repeated for another winter. But given sympathetic treatment with supplemental heat and a south window, the same plant would be in full bloom outdoors a full month earlier.

Loving Blooms: Better Late Than Never

IT'S TOO LATE, of course, but I have just finished a small bed for tall bearded irises and planted thirty-four varieties in various colors.

Their bed is six by twelve feet in land formerly sodded with Bermuda grass. It took three days to crumble each clod to get the roots out. The digging was only a foot deep. The surface was raked more or less smooth, and an inch of fully rotted horse manure was spread and then dug in. The dirt was soaked and allowed to settle for six days. A month would have been better. The irises were planted in three rows, spaced a foot apart. This means they will have to be transplanted after their first year, but the aim was to get them into the ground as soon as possible in the hope that some of them, at least, would bloom their first May. Ordinarily irises are planted from mid-July to mid-September. Earlier and later than those dates the irises are not likely to bloom their first spring, but if one is lucky and cold weather is delayed into December, they may be planted as late as early November without harm.

After planting, the rhizomes were covered with an inch of sharp sand to reduce the danger of winter heaving of the roots. While irises are hardy to cold, they are easily damaged their first winter if they have not had time to establish a full root system — hence the advice to get them into the ground by mid-September at the latest.

And yet the gardener is continually faced with the need to do things imperfectly; irises can be planted any day of the year when the ground is not frozen.

Even if they do not bloom the first spring, the flowers the second season will be better and more abundant than if they had flowered sooner, so things even out, except that few gardeners can resist the itch to see their new irises flower as soon as possible.

Elsewhere in my cat-run garden — which now is indeed a cat run, as the next-door neighbors have seven cats — it is good to see that the gentian-blue morning glory from South America, *Ipomoea acuminata,* the blue dawn flower, has finally blossomed. It has made its way up an eight-foot post and a few feet above that to collect in a tangle beneath a copper weather cock.

Some nasturtiums that faltered all summer have been covered with masses of bloom. Some of them got down into two feet of leaf mold and have produced leaves larger than the palm of hand, and these are not flowering well, but the others on a leaner diet are splendid.

All cannas, when used effectively in the general garden design, are fairly noble beasts. I have some wild ones grown from seed collected originally in South America, and these have not flowered, but another wild one, from Peru (*Canna iridiflora*), has not been without blooms since July. It was a small and seemingly weak plant from a small pot when I set it out in May, but it has now reached a bit more than seven feet in height with five stems. One panicle of flowers has seven nodding coral-rose blooms today, with another flower cluster in bud.

It is beyond question the most beautiful canna I have seen, and for several years I searched for it after seeing it in the garden of Tresco Abbey off the coast of Cornwall. It is doubtfully hardy, and its leaves are twice the size of the average canna. It grows to ten feet or so when mature, and may well be used in place of a banana plant in gardens where something smaller but equally tropical-looking is wanted.

The night jasmine growing in a barrel is showing its last blooms.

Usually it reaches its peak about Labor Day, then tapers off by mid-October, but an established plant blooms off and on from mid-May. Unfortunately it is not reliably hardy this far north. I dig mine up with a good bit of earth clinging to the roots and set it in a plastic trash bag in a cool room until May, when it is planted out again.

A plant that looks tender but is reliably hardy in Washington is the rose-colored *Clerodendrum bungei,* with flattened balls of scented bloom. I have two other kinds, scarlet and sky-blue, that are not hardy at all and are a nuisance to lug in and out.

The season for planting spring-blooming bulbs continues. October is a perfect time for crocuses, daffodils, and other spring beauties except tulips, which go in about November 11. We used to plant them on Armistice Day, but since Armistice Day is no longer on the calendar I think anytime up to Thanksgiving does well enough.

The Bloom from Buried Bulbs

FOUR FALL-BLOOMING BULBS are of minor interest unless you have them under your eye. And then they become major.

The most neglected of the group is *Sternbergia lutea,* which is like an intensely yellow crocus, only somewhat larger, thicker in substance, and more glossy in petal texture. It is not fragrant. The most economical and effective way to grow this beautiful flower is in clumps or drifts in narrow borders in front of evergreens, especially box.

But where there are plenty of bulbs to be had (as after the course of many years of increase in the garden), they can even be planted in light woodland. I used to admire them in a Virginia woods, where the road to the house ran through pines and hickories, with Michaelmas daisies and sternbergias in patches at the edge of the trees.

This flower invariably attracts attention and praise and should be seen in more gardens. The leaves emerge with the flowers, and while the flowering date may vary a little, blooms are at their best in October.

More delicate and less showy, but with more beautiful leaves, is the wild cyclamen usually called *Cyclamen neapolitanum,* but correctly *C. hederifolium.* Flowers are like the cyclamens of flower shops only much smaller, about the size of a thimble, borne on firm stems four to six inches high. The corms are circular and flat, increasing in size for decades. The larger the corm the more plentiful the flowers.

As the pink blooms fade, the stems coil and bring the seeds down to the ground, where various creatures (ants, I think) carry them off. If the gardener is lucky he soon (ten years, say) has thriving colonies with hundreds of flowers. This cyclamen begins to bloom irregularly from mid-July into November before the leaves come up.

Those leaves last in perfect condition all winter. They are the size of potato chips, only leathery and beautifully marked and blotched in shades of gray-green, all different. The bulbs used to be cheap, as they were collected from the wild, a quite naughty system. They are now far more costly but grown from seed by the nurseries.

One should never buy bulbs collected from the wild, as many are endangered and likely to become extinct. Always ask the source of the bulbs. Nurserymen always say they are seed-grown, not collected, and I think they often are telling the truth.

A true crocus that blooms in late October or early November is *Crocus speciosus,* which usually waits until a good heavy rain in October before sending up pale ivory shoots like toothpicks. These swell and soon open to flowers of soft blue-lavender. The leaves follow a few weeks later, or even with the flowers sometimes, and last until spring, when they die down. This crocus has the merit of being both the cheapest and the prettiest of the fall-blooming crocuses I have tried. It grows well in sun or light shade. I once had good drifts of it beneath an American elm and a willow oak. It does not like being overgrown with ivy.

A larger, tulip-size fall flower that otherwise resembles a crocus is colchicum. In a fit of enthusiasm I no longer understand, I once bought two hundred of them in several varieties. The off-pink *C. speciosus* is probably the most highly esteemed, but after a few years the gardener starts to admire the smaller (and more free-flowering) *C. autumnale.* Colchicums come in white and shades of purplish rose, and there are some double kinds, such as 'Waterlily'. I do not like the doubles, which usually resemble a windblown mop. All colchicums are now too costly to acquire in quantity. The leaves come up in cold weather and die down in March or April. I never thought them as unsightly as the books say, but then my colchicums always peter out after four years or so, and the leaves are therefore no problem at all.

A Garden of Choice

TAKE A PIECE OF LAND, at least in your mind, about six feet by three, and let's see what happens to it when a gardener is allowed to control it. This gardener, let us say, is not very experienced, not very rich, not endowed with total leisure. He simply has this small plot and wants to see the whole panoply of floral magnificence opened up before him in his eighteen square feet.

We start today. With a spading fork we dig along to make a trench six feet long, a foot wide, and a foot deep, and we continue until the entire eighteen square feet is admirably broken up. With our hands we break up any clods bigger than eggs. We do not want particles the size of rice, but more like gravel up to the size of eggs.

We hurry to get to the hardware store or nursery or mall shop specializing in the sale of garden supplies. We acquire eighteen pansy plants, the kind that bloom fairly freely right through the winter. We plant them a foot apart. We note how bare our little acre is. We buy eighteen daffodil bulbs. If we are well organized, we order one bulb each of eighteen kinds from a daffodil specialist, or we make do with the kinds on sale at garden centers, all of which will make a fine show.

We see that in spacing our daffodils and pansies a foot apart they seem thin indeed on the field, and besides there is a six-inch strip all the way around the perimeter in which nothing at all has been planted.

Surely there is room for — and surely there is. A few handfuls later we depart with some crocuses, the big fat yellow ones and some of the smaller kinds than that, planted right up against the ultimate edges of our plot.

No tulips? Well, hardly any. Maybe five or ten bulbs altogether. Oh, and here is one little pocket overlooked somehow, just right for three hyacinth bulbs.

But we are disciplined here. The whole point is to show how grand the spring-flowering bulbs can be when given good conditions of space and light.

During the winter we comfort ourselves with occasional flowers of crocuses and pansies. We had not known before that these small flowers are admirable for small wine glasses set beneath lamps where the heat and light keeps them open at night (outdoors they furl tight once the sun is past).

By May the daffodils are finished and the little bulbs also, but we are forbidden to cut the leaves off. A useful rule is to wait five weeks after the last flower fades, then cut the leaves back to an inch above the surface.

At this point we make a choice. The pansies will keep on blooming into August, and it seems dumb to pull them out merely to plant something in their place. But notice this: we may be tired after weeks of pansies and may start wondering if a tomato or two wouldn't produce wondrous fruits from July to November.

This past summer each of our five tomato plants produced twenty pounds of fruit. They grow well, thank you, right atop the hyacinths and other oddments of spring.

The point here is that you don't get very far down the gardening highway before hard choices must be made. Shall it be an end to pansies in favor of some new snapdragons or even a few runner beans? And if beans, should they all be some good standard kind, or is it all right to plant a few just for fun and the beauty of their flowers, like the hyacinth beans?

In gardening the question may not be whether to plant an avenue of horse chestnuts or two square feet of alyssum, but it comes to the same thing in the end. Choices must be made. You can't have everything.

Is it better to try for one grand show of tulips (giving them all the space) or to divide the space to show smaller patches of additional lovely creatures?

If we force ourselves to give each daffodil a full square foot of space we are learning the important lesson (which nobody believes until he tries it himself) that less can be more. Another good lesson right here at the beginning is that nothing is more ornamental in the garden than a superbly grown plant.

Hardly has the air begun to warm a little than a friend says his garden is devoted entirely to shallots. Someone else says life is not worth living without tuberoses. Or a grape and a fig tree. Which raises a new question: can the garden not support more than one layer of plants, with crocuses and sedums overshadowed by tulips and so-called miniature daffodils, over which some obliging rose will flop? (You can plant bulbs too close to such roses as 'The Fairy', then prune the rose unmercifully, allowing the daffodils to flower, then letting the rose grow out to cover the entire daffodil clump with blooms all summer long.)

Sooner or later you will be given some priceless plant, and the question accompanying it is where the devil it can be fitted in.

A garden is what results from years of adjustment in size and successions of enthusiasms, some longer lasting than others. (That odd twisted monster over there is all that's left from a four-year-long obsession with blueberries. Or hibiscus. Or yuccas. Or you name it.)

The garden may vary in size over the years and have no relation at all to the original little six-by-three-foot plot. And the amount of sunlight it gets changes as shrubs or even trees begin to mature. Entire sections have to be rethought and old friends given up. It is a surreal creation. As one fine gardener of England put it, his was a garden made by doing unnecessary things that he could not afford at the wrong time of the year.

You wonder after many years if any of it was worth the bother. The answer is, I think, more or less yes. All seems to be nothing but change and irregular advances and collapse, as if paying little attention to the gardener, who is seen to be far less consequential than we had supposed.

The Fifty-Year Itch

FOR FIFTY YEARS I thought (off and on) about *Allium moly,* a pretty modest yellow cousin of the onion, and when I saw it in other gardens in May I always wished I had planted a few.

The little bulbs used to cost two cents each, I think. By the time I actually bought some last fall they cost twenty cents each, but what the hell. I planted ten, and they all came up and flowered well. I wouldn't say that this fulfilled a dream of a lifetime, but I do say it's one more thing I have finally gotten around to, and I am the better man for it.

In her last year of life the elegant and down-home garden writer Katharine White planted a batch of spring-blooming bulbs as usual, and some said what a sweet affirmation of faith that was, as she would not live to see them bloom. Baloney. She planted them because, like any gardener worthy of the name, she could not resist the different shapes and hefts of small bulbs. She required, once again, to stroke the tunics (some like satin, some like glazed paper, some loose-fitting, others wrapped tight as if to face eternity in good shape).

Old gardeners have usually had the experience of not acquiring any new bulbs in some particular year, thinking they already had sufficient daffodils, tulips, and lilies to outlast time itself. But when spring came around, what a sorry and nagging little disappointment. Nothing new. Nothing to make a lady squeal.

They say time brings wisdom (a shaky proposition), but wisdom aside, time does in many cases finally bring the little yellow alliums. For a dollar or two the gardener can imagine them, snug in the lee of some old *pallida* irises. Before the end of winter some little green spears shoot up, and as the days lengthen and warm up, the flowers display themselves. All is orderly, modest, ordained from the foundation of the world, and altogether agreeable to the gardener who (if he is wise) does not reproach himself for taking decades to get the bulbs, but who compliments himself for having added one more minor monument to the garden, and who's counting years anyway?

Extravagance is never allowed in my garden. Ten alliums are enough. At the same time, if a certain bulb costs thirty-five dollars, the gardener is allowed to dodge the charge of extravagance by proclaiming (to himself) that it is an economy. Consider how much less a thirty-five-dollar bulb costs than a Rolls, how much less than a divorce or a racehorse or a mistress. It really would have been an even greater economy to acquire three instead of only one.

But the gardener is allowed to think in these new economic terms only if he has ardently longed for the extravagantly priced bulb long enough to see clearly that the extravagance was an economy all the time, and what a relief.

I used to tremble a little at the cost of certain tulips, until it dawned on me that in my former garden in Mississippi River country the tulips petered out after two years, while up here the same tulip may continue to flourish for twenty years. Thus, if the bulb cost a dollar but carried on for twenty years, it really cost only a nickel. Further, since the bulb multiplied into a small clump, the original bulb cost nothing at all, but in fact made me rich by the production of so many others over the years.

The Dutch, who lead the world in the production of superb-quality tulip bulbs, also share my economic views. They have compiled a list of those tulip varieties most likely to persist in the garden without being lifted or dipped or sprayed. I thought once of reprinting the list, but it is so long that I can summarize by saying the longevity of tulips is proved and no point rattling on about it.

My own favorite tulip is 'Jewel of Spring', which is good for years and years. I still have a few bulbs of it that have lasted a full twenty years.

And I cannot resist putting in a word for the orange parrot tulip with the imaginative name 'Orange Parrot'. It blooms so late that over the years it has produced flowers as large as grapefruits. The stem is curved and wobbly, yes, but I count it a factor of grace, and its orange coloring is applied as if Rubens and his sweetheart had devoted a weekend to it, and the flower has an intense perfume of rose–nasturtium–sweet pea.

Daffodils are even easier than tulips to justify on the budget. Buy single bulbs if the variety is costly. You don't need a clump or a large drift. Plant just one in good soil, as if you were growing vegetables. After two years dig it up and divide and replant the increase. Within four or five years you will have enough for a fine showy clump in your border and even a few to swap with some other slave.

And every year make a great point to try five or ten bulbs, or even a single bulb, of flowers new to you. I once grew a lot of ixias and got them out of my system.

You will never get crocuses out of your system, so you may as well start acquiring a few now. You still never have enough, and do not be embarrassed to crawl about on your belly among these flowers, as many are well perfumed.

And of course don't forget the alliums. No need to dawdle fifty years.

Weathering the Winter

I CAN THINK of only a few tender plants that are worth the bother of bringing indoors for the winter and setting out again in April and May. But certainly the night jasmine (*Cestrum nocturnum*), blue dawn flower (*Ipomoea acuminata*), and white potato vine (*Solanum jasminoides*) are worth the trouble of getting them safely through the winter.

If the plant is in a pot, nothing is simpler than bringing it indoors and giving it space by a sunny window and sufficient water to keep it from shriveling. This treatment works well with young potted night jasmines and the others mentioned above, but it does not work when the plant has been growing outdoors in the open ground — when it has been treated like a shrub and is too large for ordinary pots.

Such a plant may be six feet high and seven feet wide, and not every gardener has space indoors to accommodate a tub big enough for it. Such a plant is easily managed in half a whiskey barrel, and if you have an old-fashioned glass conservatory or sun porch free of frost, you have no problem; just move it in early in October and out again at the end of April.

But assuming there is no such conservatory and assuming the living room is thought unsuitable for monstrous barrels and jungles, the best thing is to dig the plant up with a spade, set it in a plastic bag of the kind used to line garbage cans, cut the branches back to three feet, and tie the bag close to the stems of the plant just above ground level.

It's hard to say how large the ball of dirt should be, but I find that if the plant with its earth clinging to the roots weighs twenty-five pounds, it will be manageable.

Enough water should be given to keep the stems from shriveling but not enough to inspire soft new growth. Let the plant dry off and lose its leaves — let it get drier than seems right. About the end of January check it, and you will find the stems are green when you scratch them, though leafless. Err on the side of too little water rather than too much. By March you can give the plant more water, sufficient to support the tender new green shoots, and all the light you can.

In a house, I know, this is not easy. Often you will wonder if the plant is going to make it. I have lost large plants by letting them get too dry, and also by keeping them too damp and luxuriant. But if you try, you will find that the plant is determined to live in spite of everything and will grow vigorously when planted in the open garden.

If the plant is so large that this method is too nerve-racking, you can leave the plant strictly alone outdoors and let the first heavy freezes of November kill it back. Then cut off the stems a few inches above ground and cover the plant with a heavy mulch, say, six or eight inches of dry leaves, and cover that with plastic or boards to keep it dry.

Instead of the mulch, you can set trash bags full of leaves all about the plant, perhaps four bags. The leaves inside the bags will rot down to good compost in time, but all you care about is the insulating effect of the leaf-filled bags. You remove them gingerly as new growth appears in April.

If all this seems too chancy and too messy, you can forget it and still give yourself a chance of success by covering the plant outdoors with a pile of evergreen branches and hoping for the best. This often works well enough with tender cannas and with tender vines.

Besides these tender plants that will endure such treatment there are regular "houseplants," such as agaves, aloes, and tropical foliage plants, that must be kept in good light and kept growing. You cannot whack them back or store them with the roots almost bone dry in plastic bags. They must be moved indoors and kept going just as if they were still in the ground outdoors — they will not take drying off.

There are days when I think I will grow only hardy plants — roses, peonies, irises, and the like — that take care of themselves outdoors. But then I know I would miss the tender plants that do so much to glorify the garden in late summer.

Every gardener must try things out for himself and hit at last on that compromise of how many night jasmines and so on he is willing to bother with.

I would not save any tender plant that I did not think was marvelous and did something (in the way of color or scent or form) that justified the yearly anxiety of pulling it safely through the winter.

You could have flowers day and night if your puritan soul can take such glory.

November

Support Groups on High

SPACE ON A BALCONY is so valuable that the gardener must not waste it, and my advice is to choose only plants that would make a lady squeal. What is squealable is, of course, up to the individual, but let us not waste time reassuring the gardener at too great length that if he has a passion for geraniums and marigolds or, for that matter, thistles and crabgrass, then that is what he should grow, and never mind what anybody else thinks.

Assuming the balcony gets sun (and don't give up without a fight if you face north, for plants are madly determined to live and will endure more deprivation than seems just), I propose that annual vines are priceless.

The totalitarian frame of mind is now so common in America that I know there are apartments in which you cannot have a dog, cat, or pet mouse or grow anything on the balcony railing. Such apartments also forbid corn bread in the kitchen, I suppose, and if you like tyranny you go along with it, but my advice, if you find yourself living in such a place, is to wake up, tell the landlord to go to hell, and move out.

Assuming you have now found a civilized place or at least a civilized landlord, you acquire a black plastic tub that holds a bushel or more of soil or a lightweight soilless planting mixture. One is tempted, if he has money, to install stone or terra-cotta tubs, but enough balconies seem to be falling off apartments these days without gardeners adding to the weight. Every prudence must be exercised. Black plastic tubs are better than whiskey barrels because they weigh less. They also are virtually invisible, calling no attention to themselves.

In one tub I applaud the white potato vine, *Solanum jasminoides,* which has clusters of small white yellow-centered flowers during the hottest season and rich green, almost ferny foliage. The vine is often said to be fragrant, though I do not find it so. From a small plant in a small pot in May it will grow to eight or ten feet by Labor Day. Given some protection in winter (it is not supposed to be hardy in Washington but often is tougher than books say it is), it will become much larger the next year. It will cover the wall of a good-size house if not killed back by cold, but the balcony gardener presumably has some shears and strength to nip away with them.

In another tub we rejoice to see either the moonflower vine, *Ipomoea alba,* which opens five-inch satin salvers on nights from July to the end of October, or else some kind of morning glory. The commonest one is 'Heavenly Blue', and it is splendid, but there is no law against investigating some of the subtropical kinds, such as *Ipomoea acuminata,* the blue dawn flower. There are also various morning glories encountered in Mexico and such places, all very agreeable (the morning glories) and mainly in tones of rose.

If there is room, you can have flowers day and night, if your puritan soul can take such glory, but one moonflower vine can turn into a very luxuriant beast indeed. I tried one seed in a two-inch pot, set down in a six-foot horse trough filled with rotted leaves. I meant to move it to a fence, but before I got around to it, the tiny plant sent its root through the pot into the compost and promptly made a mound seven feet long and three or four feet high, decked with twenty or thirty flowers at night in August. If given support (wires or poles or shrubs), the vine will reach twenty or thirty feet but is easily restrained by pinching its shoots before then.

In a third tub it is well to install a night jasmine, *Cestrum noctur-*

num, which will make a shrubby quick growth to four or seven feet (depending on sun and water, the more the better) and great foot-long panicles of tubular flowers that look like nothing much but that send forth waves of perfume on summer nights. The scent is too powerful for some gardeners, but it is perfect for those who have trouble detecting delicate scents. Unless both nose and breath are removed permanently, the night jasmine will be sensed at a distance of twenty feet, a voluptuous and possibly illegal billow of clove, syrup, and most likely some pheromone that acts on the brain. Unless one is steady, reliable, and responsible, this glorious plant should be avoided.

Here then are just three plants from among the dozens, the hundreds, the thousands, that could be tried. Some will ask, what about winter? Well, everyone to his own thing, but I suggest coming indoors on winter nights.

The Outer Limits of Inner Space

A COMMON NEUROSIS that afflicts many gardeners involves a passion for graph paper, charts, numbers, topographical maps, and lists. It is among the least painful of my own neuroses, and I commend it to all who are thinking of gardening, as well as to those who are already bogged down.

Steel tapes or, for that matter, yardsticks can measure most city gardens well enough to give the gardener an excellent idea of the extent of his estate. Furthermore, it looks better, usually, on paper than it does out the window.

If the gardener merely thinks of his garden, he has a poor (and highly exaggerated) idea of it, especially of its size. When a plant catalogue comes, the gardener (commonly in bed and comfy on a cold night) starts thinking he has a number of little spots here and there in the garden into which he could surely fit this and that plant that attracts him in the catalogue.

I have a friend who is forever ordering more clematis, because in her mind she can think how fine they would look. In due time the plants arrive, and she commonly cries for help and advice where to plant them.

"Well, that row of viburnums should be able to absorb about ten," I begin.

"The viburnums already have sixteen," she says sadly. (She got sixteen clematis without mentioning them, a year ago, and didn't cry for help, since she had places to stick them. I hear from her usually when there is not one inch anywhere for whatever plant it is that she has acquired.)

And my point is, of course, that if the garden is mapped, with everything indicated on it, then the gardener can see precisely whether or not there is space for a grove of redwoods, or whatever the latest enthusiasm happens to be.

The Cold, Hard Facts of Autumn Planting

AN ALPINE SKIER can take cold far better than a fellow working in a heated office who is suddenly dumped on a sidewalk without a coat in twenty-degree weather. Obviously, cold is both absolute and relative. At twenty below zero, the tissues of some plants will simply break, and you can say cold is an absolute menace to many plants. On the other hand, a drop from eighty to twenty above zero can work equal disaster with many other plants, even though twenty above is not all that cold. Cold is a relative menace.

This past week I planted a butterfly bush, or buddleia, a hard-to-find variety called 'Lochinch', and as I entered the house afterward a weatherman on television said a horrendous drop in temperature would occur in the next few hours.

To any experienced gardener this should suggest running back out and covering the newly planted buddleia with pine branches or a batch of oak leaves, maybe shielding it with a screen of burlap. Instead, I turned on my portable heater and ate a fine supper of fish stew and apple pie, uneasy at the driving rain and tornado warnings and all the rest of it. But I figured I would have (never mind the weatherman's alarms) a good twenty-four hours to protect the newly planted babies still in full leaf. And I was right.

Still, most gardeners can remember days on which the temperature dropped to zero within a few hours after a balmy afternoon in which the roses were still flowering.

The point is, when planting relatively tender creatures in mid-November, especially when they are in full leaf and have soft stems, it is only prudent to have protective stuff on hand. In my neighborhood somebody is always sawing down a spruce tree and piling branches in the alley. I dislike spruces and of course have none myself, but I love to take my pruning tools and fill the trunk of the car with nice twigs, about twenty inches long, from the pile in the alley. There are days I am grateful the city is not prompt in hauling off branches.

The Vices and Virtues of Climbers

THE FIRST QUESTION about any garden plant is, "Is it beautiful?" and if it isn't, then there's not much point growing it, but the next question is whether it can be grown with no more than reasonable pain.

Hardly anything is more beautiful than the climbing wild scarlet nasturtium from Chile, *Tropaeolum speciosum,* which does so well in gardens along the western coast of Scotland but which is difficult (if not impossible) here.

Once I was able to get some quite fresh seed of this brilliant creature, which looks a bit like an akebia vine studded all over with flowers the size of a thumbnail and colored the most intense saturated vermilion. I planted them the way an authority on the plant told me to and had no success except with seeds planted outdoors in September — they sprouted the next spring, and the short of it is I nursed them along for a year, but they never looked healthy or happy, even though two of them began to look a bit like a creeper.

They had to be watered every day, sometimes twice a day in hot weather. One day in September they were not watered. They died. One day without water was more than they could take. This is an example of a plant, then, that fits the description of "very difficult," not because the gardener needs to be superbly skillful but because it is almost impossible to meet the plant's requirements for cool, moist air. When I try it again, I will attempt sowing seed outdoors at the edge of azaleas under a large oak. I would like someday to flower it.

Let's turn now to a very different climber, *Polygonum aubertii,* the fleece vine or foam vine or silver lace vine, as it is called. It is a virtual weed from Asia, and without the slightest attention from the gardener it grows to forty feet in a couple of years. It will cover a barn. It gets no fungus or other diseases that I can see, and no bugs bother it. It does not need spraying or fertilizing or watering in dry spells. It needs no protection in winter.

More than that, it is a plant of quite flawless beauty. The effect in bloom is of a green mantle overlaid with a dense filigree of muted silver-white, and there is a slight scent. At night, by the light of the moon (or an alley lamppost), it is magical.

Furthermore, it starts blooming in May, tapers off a bit in hot weather, and starts blooming again with a passion about Labor Day, continuing into October, a time when few things in the garden are at their best.

There is some prejudice, I am sorry to notice, against this superb plant because any fool can grow it to perfection, and I suppose because it is not rare.

There is an unattractive aspect of refinement in humans, by which they undervalue and almost distrust lavish splendor. Shakespeare and Balzac are often ignored (when it comes to actually reading them) when lesser writers are esteemed. This is because one is sometimes awed by writers so obviously prolific and remarkable. Perhaps there is some human instinct for coziness or miniature wonders, to the detriment of volcanic splendors.

The great polygonum has suffered from the refined gardener's distrust of things that are trouble-free, lavish, and heedless of the gardener's futzing about with serums and hot towels, as it were.

Another great climber subject to the same prejudice is the Boston ivy, *Parthenocissus tricuspidata*. It goes without saying that we gardeners often use such great plants in the worst possible way. The Boston ivy will grow right over all the windows of a house, obscuring everything in a monotonous skin of green leaves. But when grown up a tree, hanging down in huge garlands of foliage (which turn crimson in the fall), it is a magnificent thing to see.

Likewise the polygonum can be bad on a three-foot-high fence between the rose garden and the asparagus beds. It does not want to sit on such a fence neat and prim; it wants (and is determined) to fling itself high and wide.

I grow it in a space ten feet high and twelve feet long, and it is almost impossible to keep it from covering every square inch. It would be much better planted where it could go fifteen feet up and fifty feet wide, and even then you would have to keep an eye on it.

But suppose you have a high fence a hundred feet long. There it would be splendid. The surprising thing is that a plant of such vigor should have flowers of such delicacy. It is a climber of unsurpassed beauty. It only needs to be placed where its exuberant growth is a virtue and not a vice.

Be It Blotch or Brilliance . . .

✿ VARIEGATED LEAVES can be beautiful, and they can also give quite a messy, disordered effect in the garden if used lavishly or without that fine discrimination that you and I always display. In a word, one gardener's great mess is another gardener's exciting artistry. If you can't stand leaves that are striped, marbled, mottled, or blotched with silver, white, or yellow, then you will forget about plants with variegated foliage.

For a long time I disapproved of such foliage, saying it looked like disease to me. What brought me around first was the variegated Italian arum, which varies somewhat, some plants being more marbled in the leaf than others. It grows readily from seed, though such small beasts as ants are probably responsible for stealing the brilliant orange-red seeds once they drop to the ground.

On a visit to England I once saw a beautiful form of the common yellow swamp iris with gold leaves. In this plant the "variegation" is not marbling or blotches or stripes; instead the entire leaf is rich yellow, at least in spring, but the color turns to green about July.

For some reason I could not find this gold form in America, though I know there is a German variety of some brilliance, and I once acquired it in a weak plant that did not survive a Washington heat spell. At last I found a gold form, but it is not showy in the fall; the yellow coloring is much subdued, though still present to some extent.

A nurseryman provided me with another beautiful iris with silver-white striped leaves, a variegated form of *Iris ensata,* which used to be called *I. kaempferi.* I grow both these irises in pots, though they are perfectly hardy and would do better in the open ground, because I can keep an eye on them, and they will not be swamped with weeds. The variegated plant that has given me most pleasure over the years is the variegated sweet flag. This sounds like an iris but it's not. It's a totally different kettle of fish, *Acorus calamus variegatus.* Its leaves resemble those of a Japanese iris, more or less, but unlike the iris, this plant bears little conelike green flowers that protrude from the leaf sheaves. Odd and beautiful.

There are dozens — or hundreds, maybe thousands — of plants that have variegated leaves, and the gardener owes it to himself to try a couple. Often one's opinion of a plant changes utterly when one grows the plant and comes to know it intimately.

To remind us that rarity is one thing and beauty is another, I remind you that no variegated plant is more brilliant than the common gardener's garters, which is rather a weed in good soil.

The acorus or sweet flag, by the way, was cut and used as a strewing herb on the floors of Tudor palaces, though as far as I can tell it was only the green form, not the white-striped form, that was used. The roots smell like tangerines when cut.

I have never had enough of my striped form to cut the roots for their fragrance. It is one of those plants that people like most to beg a root of. We ought not be stingy, but in an unworthy way I hate to see the sweet flag go and (also unworthily) try to hint that it is not a very good plant really and flops about untidily. Often, however, the intending borrower refuses to be discouraged, and there goes another snippet.

When Perfect Isn't Good Enough

THERE MUST BE a big root somewhere. The shady leaf-mold peat-moss spot, shaded from the south by a large osmanthus bush, is ideal for a honeysuckle ('Late Dutch') and a beautiful small evergreen vine, *Kadsura japonica*.

It is ideal except that it is all wrong. I have to water, even in the fall and even when other plants need no water. Must be a big root. Just across the walk from this spot is a site perfect for the scarlet honeysuckle. Except it is impossible to keep it alive there; the drainage is too poor. How can the drainage be poor? It's at the top of a slope. I mention these two spots, seemingly perfect, to show that things are going on in the garden we do not notice on the surface.

Yet a third perfect spot for a viburnum is so bad I can barely keep the plant alive. I did find out what's wrong there — a leak from gas mains. My view is that the whole city sits atop leaking water and gas mains, and there are actually buried rocks in many gardens, a thing I never heard of in my life. Where I grew up you could dig down thirty feet and hit nothing except alluvial loam or loess. So imagine my surprise at rocks. It was very like meeting a dinosaur.

There are two ways to deal with plants that have been put in bad sites that seemed ideal at the time of planting. The sensible way is to move the plant. That will never do, of course, and the second way is to coddle the plant along, giving supplements of one kind or another.

So I get out there and water the kadsura. I withhold water from the smilax (it sits in what is almost a sump hole). I give leaf mold and I scratch lightly. In this way the things survive, somewhat like a great-aunt who has had a heart condition for the past eighty-three years of fragile health.

Three times recently — the mention of scarlet honeysuckle reminds me — I have seen asinine warnings in print against the plant, one of the greatest garden treasures of our country. It is said in all these warnings that this honeysuckle can be a terrible pest and will kill young trees and get quite out of hand. This is not so.

The honeysuckle to be feared is the Japanese honeysuckle, 'Hall's Variety', which was imported in the last century and which has escaped to become a scourge. It has white flowers that turn yellow with age. It is intensely fragrant, a very fine scent. It is almost evergreen.

But the scarlet honeysuckle, *Lonicera sempervirens,* is a modest twiner native to our own woods, not that you ever see it except in gardens. Its clusters of little scarlet trumpets have no scent, a sad defect, but it is the most brilliant of the honeysuckles. George Washington apparently made much of it on the arcades of his house, Mount Vernon, and I never met anybody who didn't think it beautiful. The unfortunate truth is that some of the scolds who love to warn everybody about everything do not know one honeysuckle from another, and do not even know there are about ten kinds that might be tried in gardens.

The great Burmese honeysuckle, which is not hardy except in nearly frost-free places and is far too tender to grow outdoors in Washington, is exactly the kind of plant the gardener lusts after. Its trumpets are heavy as wax, powerfully scented, and the gardener thinks now *there* is a honeysuckle. Each flower is about six inches long. But then you notice that the old flowers turn yellow and brown and rot on the vine. And the perfume, which seems so grand at first, is cloying. So I do not regret the lack of that honeysuckle nearly as much as I did a few years ago.

The scarlet honeysuckle has a variant that is solid yellow and also scentless.

Even the vicious Hall's honeysuckle can be a beautiful garden plant when given attention and not allowed to take over the garden. It can be clipped and grown tight against an old tree trunk or even on a wire frame or fence. But if it is allowed to go its own way, it will kill out shrubs and young trees. Since it is a notable pest, perhaps we're lucky the flowers are so handsome and the perfume so sweet. But for most gardeners, it is best left out of the garden. I feel this the more keenly when I have almost bled to death pulling it off mahonia bushes.

But back to those plants that have been set in sites they do not like. I will not move my Dutch honeysuckle or kadsura because I want those two plants just where they are. I'm sorry they don't like it, sorry the spot is too dry, but I gave much thought to what I wanted there and they must make do. They can join the world like the rest of us.

But I do know I have to water more than seems just to me. I know I have to dole out little light mulches of very well rotted manure, which I hand out like gold, stingily. I do not begrudge this artificial coddling of both plants any more than I begrudge the big agaves that have to come indoors every winter.

Of course, if I had known the problems then as I know them now, I would have excavated a Volkswagen-sized hole and filled it with new dirt laced with rotted leaves and peat moss. But now the plants are established and I don't want to start over. I must now endure the wasteful process of trying to ameliorate a bad condition when it would have been easier to change that condition before planting the vines.

It's not that we don't learn. It's that the world is hard.

Among the Berry Best of Bushes

❁ BESIDES THE GREAT TRIBES of shrubs notable for berries, such as hollies and viburnums, there are lesser-known berried plants, some showy and some full of interest even with black fruit.

I rarely see the Carolina moonseed, *Cocculus carolinus,* though it grows like a weed and, come to think of it, is a weed. All the same, I once saw an eight-foot-high trellis many feet long that was devoted entirely to 'Paul's Scarlet', that climbing rose of undeniable beauty and brilliance for all its faults (it is scentless, has a short season of flower, is not free of black spot, and has a gawky habit of growth). Among the roses the moonseed had established itself, and in fall when (thanks to black spot) the rose was almost leafless, the bright red berries, like crimson glass beads, made a brave show.

Some gardeners do not like black fruit, but I never tire of admiring old plants of common ivy when they have reached the height of their support and have formed woody side branches that flower in September. The greenish-white, inconspicuous flowers are followed by rock-hard black berries, dull in finish but quite handsome. Of course they will never do if the gardener has a taste for neon.

Equally beautiful is the Southern smilax or Jackson vine, *Smilax smallii.* This has thorny stems, almost invisible flowers, and black berries bigger than peas. It sends out wiry tendrils that lash the pale stems to wire or trellis or other shrubs, depending on what it can find for support. The leaves are lance-shaped, highly polished, and evergreen, and the stems are limp enough that it is (or was) used everywhere for garlands or for trails of greenery down banquet tables. It may have been a law in the South, formerly, that no occasion grander than a beer bust could be held without a few bushels of smilax hung about.

The callicarpas, which have no common name except beautyberry, which is rather disgusting to my mind, make moderate bushes up to six feet or so. The leaves are coarse and uninteresting but have the merit of dropping early in the fall, to reveal pale stems encrusted every few inches with masses of violet berries. There are several kinds, and the wild one I used to see in dry woodlands is as handsome as any. The callicarpas are outstanding, and possibly unique, in the color of their fruit, visible at some distance.

The Virginia creeper and the Boston ivy (both of them forms of *Parthenocissus*) are grown for their luxuriant leafage and their vigor.

They could cover the Capitol with dense green if planted there and allowed to grow unhindered. I was very sorry once to see beautiful old brickwork at Sutton Court attacked by these climbers. They are beautiful plants, but they obscure architectural detail. They should be grown on otherwise ugly fences or up trees, where they can trail down leafy garlands here and there.

But, not to wander, the clusters of dull light blue fruit are pleasant to see as well. The only trouble is that birds eat the berries, and I sometimes think every one sprouts. Even more beautiful in fruit is the porcelain berry, *Ampelopsis brevipedunculatus,* a long name that means nothing more alarming than that the berries are borne on very short stalks or peduncles. These berries are luminous bright blue. A plant in fruit is irresistible. The trouble is that it too seeds all over the place and is so lush in growth that it will kill any unfortunate shrub in its way. Still, when controlled, few vines are as beautiful.

More restrained and even more beautiful in leaf is *Parthenocissus henryana,* the five-fingered leaves of which are almost velvety in effect (though smooth to the touch). They are salmon-colored when new, turning to soft green with sometimes a mysterious red cast to them, and with a pale stripe down the center of each leaflet. It is a better choice than all the others if the gardener does not wish to spend his life whacking vines.

The euonymus tribe has many species with beautiful fruit. My own favorite is the winged euonymus, with corky ridges running along the stems. This *E. alata* is impressive as a plant eight feet high and fifteen feet wide, and is a glory in late November (or as early as October in some places) when the leaves turn a soft but luminous red. Some call it Venetian red. If you think of scarlet overlaid with gray velvet, then the velvet wiped off — that is absurd, but the point is that these leaves are of a curious tone. Anyway, when they drop, the scarlet waxy seeds are seen, and while they fall rather quickly, there are sometimes days when the fruit alone is showy.

There are both American and European euonymus — please do not ask me to say euonymuses — that have fleshy, rose-colored fruits the size of butter beans. The American one is sometimes called hearts bustin' with love, and apparently in need of oxygen, as the color is a bit purplish. For some years I have grown a garden variety called 'Red Cascade', which blooms and grows like mad, suckering all over the place, but without fruit. It clearly needs another euonymus to pollinate it.

The same is true of most hollies, but there are so many hollies about that you can get away with planting only a fruiting holly, the female form, as there is enough pollen (from the male forms) that berries will set even if you do not plant a male holly near. That saves space, though the truth is that male hollies with no fruit are as handsome (sometimes even handsomer in foliage) as the female forms with berries.

Birds do not like them in some years but in other winters they are esteemed.

December

The Budding Holly Story

LATE NOVEMBER can be a beautiful time and it can also be gray and cold. Many a Thanksgiving Day brings shirt-sleeve weather, and often our skies are still brilliant blue. At no other season are berries so greatly appreciated, and a word about them is overdue.

First, there are the hollies. Not only is the common American holly, *Ilex opaca,* in its glory now, but many other neglected members of this grand genus are notable garden shrubs or trees. The American holly is variable, and several hundred varieties may be had by gardeners who explore catalogues and nurseries. These trees vary in leaf shape, leaf color, growth habit, and fruit (some fruit heavily, some never fruit but are valuable as pollinators).

There are many hybrid hollies, as well as wild kinds from Asia and Europe. Among the hybrids is 'Foster No. 2', a small tree with long narrow leaves and, in good years, so many bright red berries the branches are bent down. It is valuable for its narrow upright growth, and even better than most other hollies it bears pruning and may be kept narrow for thirty years or more with little effort.

One of the glossiest dark hollies, with small curved and spiny leaves, is Father Perny's holly, *Ilex pernyi,* and there are several hybrids from it, handsome in fruit and stunning in foliage.

Very popular and good hybrid hollies are the group called the Meserve hybrids. These have very dark, glossy leaves and rather large, bright red berries. The leaves may seem almost blue-black or green-black, and they seem rather slow-growing, which is a merit in small gardens.

The English holly grows admirably in the capital and, like the American holly, it is known in endless variety. Gardeners who like variegated leaves will find them in this group, the deep glossy green heavily blotched with yellow or white. The English hollies fail in much of middle America but are at home in the Middle Atlantic and Pacific Northwest regions.

The yaupon (*Ilex vomitoria*) is an American native, most at home from Norfolk south but worth trying in Washington. The danger is that in some unspeakable winter it may be killed, and this sets gardeners off in unattractive ways. It makes a fine hedge, as most evergreen hollies do. Its narrow, smooth leaves often have a yellowish cast, and the small red berries are pleasant if not very showy. Like most red-berried hollies the yaupon can be found with yellow berries. The name *vomitoria* comes from the high caffeine content of its leaves, which can be boiled into a black liquid and drunk, producing vomiting. I tried them once with no result, but various Indian tribes used the drink in communal ceremonies.

There are yet other lesser-known native evergreen hollies, as well as the much neglected native deciduous hollies. One of the most beautiful of these is *Ilex decidua*, which you find in rich lowlands of the Lower Mississippi. After a hard freeze the leaves blacken and fall, leaving the brown stems strung with what seem like millions of red or yellow berries. It is not so widely grown as *Ilex verticillata*, another deciduous native, but no plant can be more striking in late November than *I. decidua*.

There are many other fine hollies too numerous to mention in a general note like this, but all are worth growing. It is surprising that so few gardeners of the lazy sort do not settle for a holly grove on a small scale.

Often in December I have stopped the car and walked into an old holly grove along the great river where the only other plants were the red cedar, *Juniperus virginiana*, and even on a cold windy gray day the air is still and almost warm inside the grove. My favorite one was sawed down one year by vandals, who trucked off the branches for Christmas sales in Chicago.

The great tribe of viburnums is now recognized for its outstanding beauty and adaptability in the garden. Some viburnums are treasured mainly for their flowers, such as 'Mariesii' and *V. juddii*, but others that are less showy in flower are redeemed by magnificent displays of fruit. Many viburnums have colored leaves in November, and even the flowering kinds, such as the two mentioned, turn golden-orange-bronze or crimson, respectively.

Some viburnums grow to the size of dogwoods, but others are easier to site in the small garden, especially the tea viburnum, *V. setigerum*. I grow it in poor, dry soil, a thing all viburnums abhor, and I do this partly to keep the plants smaller than an old lilac. This viburnum has slender branches that arch over a bit from the weight of red berries in clusters. There is a hint of orange in that red, giving brilliance. Some years it colors as early as late summer, and if there are hard freezes in November the fruit withers and softens.

The same is true of Wright's viburnum, *V. wrightii*. Its fruit is dark translucent crimson, not showy unless carefully sited, as against a white wall, where the clusters are stunning. It too rarely preserves its fruit past early December, but mockingbirds eat them.

They also eat small crab apples, such as the most beautiful of all crab apples for the small garden, *Malus sargentii*. This is a rounded, nearly globular small tree or shrub with fragrant white flowers in April and smooth, red, raisin-size fruit that only shows up well after a hard freeze has made the leaves drop. The fruit lasts until spring.

One of the truly dazzling berried shrubs is the common evergreen *Nandina domestica*, said to be planted near tea houses in Japan, with small twiggy growths said to be useful as toothpicks. I have tried them, but as I am not sure how to use toothpicks I cannot vouch for their value. I can vouch for the beauty of their great panicles, more than a foot long, of scarlet berries that last all winter and even to May. Birds do not like them in some years, but in other winters they are esteemed. An old nandina bush with an inch of snow on it, with cardinals sitting on the branches pecking at the fruit, is a fine thing to see in January.

The Latest Dirt on the Garden's Doings

HYACINTHS SHOULD BE PLANTED in October, in friable, rich, well-dug earth that crumbles easily when rubbed in the fist. So sue me. I did the best I could, and when the beautiful white hyacinth 'Carnegie' finally got planted within shouting distance of Christmas, the earth was not quite soggy but wetter than damp.

Several weeks before, I planted other hyacinths properly and dug the planting site for 'Carnegie', which was to be planted the next day. Then things came up. So shoot me. At least I kept the bulbs well ventilated and cool before planting.

I mention this not to glorify sloth but to reveal the truth, that the gardener's life is not a perfect hyacinth bed but a life of unexpected failures and sorrows, somewhat redeemed by unexpected and utterly accidental triumphs. Not that I have any to report today. Curiously, squirrels have ignored a heavy fall of acorns, or at least have left fallen ones all over the sidewalk instead of cleaning them up promptly. They did bury a number of them in a small bed where I dug up the great angel's-trumpets for the winter (they were not great at all last summer, but surely they will take off when planted outdoors again come May) and where the soil was well worked and friable.

Today I see a squirrel digging there to retrieve some acorns — and, as usual, not finding them but discovering my valued forms of the wild *Crocus tomasinianus.*

This is the first year the squirrels have shown an interest in the small scarlet fruits of such roses as 'Seagull', 'Will Scarlet', and 'Ginny', all of them notable for clusters of fruit following their clusters of flowers. Late this fall the garden walk was thick with hulls of the rose hips — evidently it is only the seeds that are eaten. Why squirrels never ate them before but descended on them mightily this year I do not know. Neither do I know why they did not eat a single tomato last summer, though two years earlier I had to cover the plants with nets.

I have put up a house for bats. It hangs from a bracket set at the apex of a garage gable. Probably it will prove ideal for wasps, and needless to say no bat has so much as looked at it. Susan Davis has quantities of bats at her place a few miles distant. Could newly weaned bats be moved?

Some months ago I had to cancel a talk in Lawrence, Kansas, and a television crew arrived here to show, I suppose, that I was seriously off my feed and could not travel. We waddled about the garden, which was ill kempt. Months later I finally screwed up the courage to play the tape of this ill-considered venture, and as I had feared (in my initial protests at the very idea of television), it showed me as rather fat and far from youthful. Talk about distortions. But the star of the program was a mockingbird, singing in top form at top volume. Yet at the time of the filming we were unaware of so sweet a songster as we galumphed about. The moral is clear enough, that most of the beauty of a garden we are oblivious to, being preoccupied with absurd concerns about bugs on the nasturtiums or a certain rounding out of the body. And I will say this for the garden in that film, and it's about all I can say for it: it was rather funny, and the growth was as luxuriant as a jungle — it showed a place where mockingbirds sing like mad.

My yellow narcissus in pebbles, 'Grand Soleil d'Or', is not coming along nearly as well as expected. But then I never thought it would. In time, perhaps. In time. That's a good phrase for the gardener to get used to from the very beginning.

The Beauty of Natural Selection

❀ NOW THE FULL BEAUTY of common holly, common ivy, and almost all bamboos is seen in perfection, and I hope I never lose my admiration for them merely because they are foolproof and "ordinary." Nothing in any garden is more beautiful than ivy when it reaches the top of its support and begins to branch and flower (in September) and then bear its clusters of black berries.

A good addition to the usual ivy is the Persian ivy, *Hedera colchica*, with larger, heart-shaped leaves, along with its gold-variegated forms. In England these gold-blotched kinds, such as 'Paddy's Pride', are overdone. They are best used only where they can stand alone, not as a background to colorful flowers.

Indoors I keep a half-despairing eye on the large agaves, or century plants. It is about time for them to split open their terra-cotta pots. I hate the thought of heavy wooden tubs or even those useful black plastic tubs, but the thought of giving up these old plant friends is too painful to dwell on.

By my bed is a sorry little collection of half-dead plants (which will be fine once they can go outdoors again at the end of April) that give me the greatest pleasure but that remind me how ignorant we are about the deep mysteries of life.

Side by side are two six-inch pots. One holds *Furcraea macdougalii* from Oaxaca and the other is home to *Puya mirabilis* from South America. Most puyas dwell in the Andes and, like most other South American plants, are quite unsuitable for East Coast gardens. Both plants are basal rosettes; that is, all the leaves come from one point, very like yuccas or agaves. The leaves of both are succulent and armed along the margins with small spines. What intrigues me is that the furcraea spines point up and the puya spines point down.

You can run your hand freely along the edge of the leaf of each plant, as long as you rub in the right direction. Why does one plant seem to encourage small beasts to the center of the plant while the other does just the opposite?

The agaves also have spines along the leaf edges, but these stick straight out, not downward or upward. There is some reason for all these variations, but I have no idea what.

Many devices in nature are, if not altogether random, at least experimental, as if plants liked to play and romp a bit. The variations are within certain limits. The spines can be of different sizes and may point always in some particular direction, but they remain spines.

It used to be thought that variations occurred at random, any which way, and that they made no difference and had no significance unless they conferred some advantage to survival (in which case that variation soon became general) or else proved a disadvantage to the plant (in which case the variation soon died out in competition with plants better adapted to their environment).

The suspicion grows, however, that in nature the concept of any-which-way variation may be too simple an explanation. Roger Lewin's arresting new book, *Complexity*, deals with chaos and pattern, making everybody quite uneasy and challenging many comfortable assumptions we inherited from the last century without providing any new comfort at all, except such a chilly one as may be found in the pursuit of truth.

Apart from their astounding beauty and variety of form and color, plants hold many profound secrets. Plants, after all, were the foundation laboratory for Darwin's great proofs in the field of natural selection and the evolution of new species. If Darwin were at my house, he would have a good idea why the spines of my South American babies behave as they do, and in years to come these variations will be seen far more clearly than now.

When I peer about my little garden, which is sometimes so beautiful, I never admire this plant or that without a certain awe that beneath the surface and structural beauty that even the coarsest human eye can see lies a creative dynamic truth at the heart of all life that is still hidden from simple men like me but that will one day be clear to all.

The Imperfect Gardener

THE COMMONEST BAD MISTAKES made by gardeners, as I judge from my own experience, are these:

Failure to enclose the garden with shrub screens, hedges, walls, fences, and such, with the result that the scene never looks finished, no matter how well things are growing or how many things are in flower.

Planting too closely. No gardener thinks time will pass and plants will grow. Even slow growers like box increase in bulk surprisingly, in surprisingly few years.

Ignoring the tremendous effect of small flowers massed. Instead, the gardener too often plants varieties with large individual flowers that show up far less well than varieties with much smaller flowers but more of them.

Inability to focus on one thing at a time. There are only so many weeks a year, and most shrubs flower for at least two weeks, so the task of planting the most beautiful or interesting things for each season is not too burdensome. But the gardener will not focus on such seasons as, say, early July, then plant things together that look fine then.

The fault of hoping always to find varieties that bloom the longest. Thus, the gardener must have roses that bloom from May to November, deploring peonies, lilacs, fall crocuses, and other flowers that come in one great burst, then shut up shop for the rest of the year.

I say nothing of many other faults, such as letting the fence lean instead of repairing it promptly or leaving empty pots at the side of the walk instead of storing them neatly in the garage.

One of the most startling demonstrations in all gardening is to watch Americans prowling about the celebrated gardens of England. They moan and croon and say they could never achieve such effects back in America, because the English climate is so favorable, so mild. In this they are totally wrong. England has a dreadful climate, hardly any sun and, surprisingly, not enough rain, either. Things grow slowly there. It is July before things truly get going, and they peter out in September.

Most of the plants admired in those island gardens are readily grown in Washington and other moderate regions of our country, and even in the Plains states luxuriant effects can be had from quite hardy plants.

I have seen Americans in England falling into fits over such roses as 'Seagull', or fainting in Paris over a similar rose, 'Thalia'. The trouble is not that such things grow better abroad than here but that here the gardener would not dream of planting them. The gardener here plants some climbing rose, brand-new, that is supposed to be showy and constant, then wonders why, a few years later, it does not really give the effect he wants.

Such roses as 'Seagull', with flowers only an inch or so wide, come in great clusters and emit heady perfume. They make a tremendous show for two or three weeks. They do not bloom again till the following spring, and this is argued against planting them.

Then why do Americans have such fits over English gardens, where such roses are as common as they are rare in America? I could understand someone's not liking 'Seagull', or any other particular rose, but I do not understand why the gardener refuses to plant it here, then goes off his rocker when he sees it abroad.

I have seen public rose gardens (and it's a scandal there is none of consequence in Washington) in full bloom that give no idea of the beauty of the rose. All the bushes are in bloom, but the viewer is not impressed.

Then what a revelation it is to visit the great public garden in Paris, the Roseraie de l'Haÿ, at the end of June. For the first time many an American gardener begins to see walls of roses, fountains of roses, arches of roses, and to comprehend that the rose, all by itself, can equal in flamboyance a garden of massed azaleas.

But when you investigate the varieties that produce the amazing walls and hummocks of color you find there are eighty huge plants of 'Alexandre Girault' on two-story trellises across the back of the garden. This is a two-inch rose that blooms only once a year, and its color is more rose than red, and not at all bright. Yet when massed it is gorgeous enough.

You may race over to see what those enormous standards are, those small "trees" on a single trunk with heads six feet across, an unbelievable mass of soft blush-pink flower. You are surprised to see it is nothing but that excellent American rose 'New Dawn', grown in this form to provide thousands of roses up at eye level, above the massed bedding roses and below the tall screens of roses that reach to the sky.

No gardener can pass by the crescent of pylons fifteen feet high, smothered with roses top to bottom and alternating soft pink and red. They are endlessly photographed and envied. Yet the two roses are 'Paul's Scarlet Climber' and 'Mrs. F. W. Flight'. Paul's rose is certainly everywhere in America, though planted less often than formerly. It has no scent, it is gawky if not trained to stay put on wall or fence (or pillar), Its foliage is not handsome, it gets black spot, and it blooms only once a year.

And as for 'Mrs. Flight', I know of no source for this rose in America or England. Yet seeing it at the Roseraie de l'Haÿ will stop any gardener in his tracks. It is hardly new, though now very rare, as it came out in 1906.

As for such now-despised roses as 'American Pillar', 'Evangeline', and 'Dorothy Perkins' (all bred in America, of course), they are the main glory of this famous garden, even though most of them have flowers an inch across. There they are with other small-flowered roses such as 'Violette' (one of those purple roses sadly ignored and rarely sold in our country), all of them solid in flower from ground to top of arch. To walk beneath those endless arches, some white, some pink, some purple, some scarlet, is an excitement not to be found in our gardens.

The effects of all these in Paris come at the cost of a lot of labor, pruning and tying. I am not saying we should all concentrate on these once-flowering graceful roses. I do say that these rather de-spised and certainly neglected roses are the ones used in that garden, the ones that amaze Americans, though Americans stopped growing them by 1920.

You cannot get that effect of being walled in by billions of roses from the stiff climbers we all choose. Such fine modern climbers as 'Compassion' (to mention the greatest first) or 'Golden Showers' or the rich, magnificent red 'Don Juan' will never present that element of lavish color that the more modest ramblers will show.

Just this one instance of almost tiny rose flowers' producing more color (and more graceful and more delicate billows of it) than our best large-flowered roses should make the point: do not be seduced too often by large, showy varieties at the cost of neglecting small-flowered kinds, and do not be snookered too far by the (often illusory) blessing of "continual flowering" varieties to the neglect of those that bloom only once a year for a few days but that you will remember (even if you see them in Paris only once) the rest of your life.

Potted Perspicacity

MY EXPERIENCE WITH HOUSEPLANTS — those that live outdoors from May to October — is that they survive best when kept dry, to the point of wilting, and of course no fertilizer.

A senior plant is an agave in a fourteen-inch pot that was rescued several years ago from an alley where it had been thrown, presumably by somebody not fond of agaves. Since then it has had two offsets that were separated and that now occupy twelve-inch pots. The needle spines at the tips of the leaves, which could put a dog's eye out (or a person's, of course), are cut off with scissors, though nothing can be done about the spines along the leaf edges.

I give each big agave a cup of water about every two months. Lugging the plants in and out in season is a nuisance, but the trick is to have the earth quite dry and therefore less weighty and to hold the pot tight against the chest. Naturally, any ancient copper pots hanging on the wall in the kitchen (through which I go to the back door) manage to get snagged by the long firm agave leaves, so there is a good bit of noise.

I got rid of a six-inch pot of agaves with four small plants in it when an electrician admired it recently. You can always find homes if you get too many.

In more congenial or at least warmer climates the agave makes a rosette six feet high or more and occupies a space ten feet across. In time the plant blooms on a great stalk perhaps twenty feet high, then dies, and you start over from offsets. I give the plants as much sun as I can indoors, but they survive well without any direct sun as long as they are kept on the dry side.

I have lost a great treasure, *Furcraea longaeva,* which looks halfway between an agave and a yucca. I had raised it from a seedling smaller than my thumb, and it had made a glorious green rosette with arching leaves about two feet long. But it fell off the rim of a fish pool and was in the water two days. I thought surely it would recover, but it rotted almost instantly and never showed any signs of life from the roots.

About twenty years ago I bought a little *Dracaena marginata* in a four-inch pot for sixty-nine cents. It now has several stems and is about seven feet high in its twelve-inch pot. It would be much larger except I keep it starved and pot-bound. Outdoors in summer it happily sends roots into the surrounding earth, but when I bring the pot indoors I cut them off. The same is true of another foliage plant or two. All those that survive over the years are able to manage with little light and water. A fiddle-leaf fig protests to the point of dying back and looking dead, at which point it gets mouth-to-mouth, as you might say. It has remained small, as you might guess, in its ten-inch pot.

Starting in mid-December I venture into the basement every few days to see if the amaryllis bulbs show signs of life. They are kept in pots all year long and spend the warm months at the foot of an east-facing fence. The pots sit in a shallow trench and are watered perhaps once a month. They should have a bit of fertilizer during the summer but don't get it. My experience is that they want no more than half a day of sun when outdoors.

Once I see signs of a sprouting leaf in the basement, the pots come up and sit on a great tray in a south window. I water them cautiously until I see they are really growing, then I keep the soil barely damp.

The only tricky time for these splendid South African bulbs (*Hippeastrum* is the botanical name usually given them, but they are the common big amaryllis sold at garden shops) is the period between the fading of the flowers and the month of May, when they go outdoors. The leaves are large and floppy, and the gardener's interest flags. The pots must be kept in sunlight and the bulbs must be given plenty of water.

The medicine cabinet contains a little jar of mud and water in which three seeds of *Euryale* repose. That is the great water planter, a water lily that boasts ferocious spines on its three-foot-wide leaves. The seeds still seem firm, but they have been there for three years now. Every week or so I check the water when I shave. No telling what problems would arise if they ever sprouted and the plant began to grow. I have no space for it in the outdoor pool but could fit it in somehow. In the winter, however, I do not need washtub-size leaves covered with spines. The house has pretty much filled up with winter visitors, an odd situation for a man who rather dislikes houseplants. Except, of course, my babies that need shelter.

In Gardening, Timing Is the Key

WHEN YOU FIRST START to garden you usually have no idea what the real delights are going to be. You generally suppose the joy will come from raising the first dahlia bigger than a washtub or producing a rose seven inches across. These are heady highs, of course. But they overlook the element of time. Time, you might almost say, is what gardening is about.

It's one thing — and a fine one — to see the leaves fall in November and the first crocus in January and the snowdrops on February 4 and the azaleas on April 15 and so on and on, the first year you see all this.

It's another and more resonant thing the thirtieth time you see it. A certain daffodil opens on March 4, and you are dumbfounded. Always before it opened on March 15 or 16, not varying year after year. So why is it blooming so much earlier this year? The weather and temperatures give no clue. Now this makes the flower much more engaging than it would be had you not watched it opening on March 15 for the last twenty years.

The roses come and go. At first you think, when June comes and the bush is out of bloom, that an eternity will pass before next May when it blooms again. But after a few years you conclude that 'Agnes', say, is worth growing even if it blooms only once a year.

It is very like discovering that youth does not last or come around on schedule every year. At first it is a shock. But if you are reasonably lucky, as I was, you like getting older. You don't have to live through all that youthful bother again, and the future may well be novel and more agreeable than the past.

In the garden, at least, you soon grow almost sick of flowers that bloom endlessly. I love the petunias, the wild-looking off-white and pale lavender ones that keep popping up from self-sown seed. They always look cheerful in the heat, they smell just fine, and they never look worn out and bedraggled. Besides, their color is soft and they don't scream at you.

But floribunda roses can become boring after a while; so can marigolds. They are nice enough, it's just that after a few months you wish they would look a little different.

It is otherwise when the snowdrops bloom. Wow. Look at that. Right through the snow. Nobody ever gets bored with snowdrops or crocuses. Or the strange flower of the jack-in-the-pulpit or the marbled Italian arum. It only lasts a few days, then is gone, and is not showy even for the four days it's in bloom. But what a pleasure to see it, when its brief day comes.

Azaleas are an example of flowers that finish blooming just about the time I get sick of looking at them. For some people, azaleas bloom too long, but for me they hit it just about right. I have never liked those late azaleas of May and June; by then I have had a bellyful. But when April comes around again, the azaleas are greeted like long-lost friends. So there is something to be said for not being gorgeous for so long that everybody loses interest.

The coming and going of flowers, the rise and fall of plants, are of utmost importance in the pleasure of gardening, far more than the young gardener might think. That gardener has not lived until he has experienced the death of a magnolia or a yew or a camellia that he had thought would be there forever. What a shock. But after it happens a few times the gardener no longer goes to pieces. It's the way life is, and the gardener learns that life really does go on.

Sometimes you will plant a pecan nut, just for the hell of it, and then marvel when a violent storm snaps the crown off it fifty years later and (if the innings hold) how a new leader develops and the tree looks none the worse for wear at sixty years. A plant means one thing to you if you buy a house and find a hundred-year-old oak, a wonderful bit of luck. But it means something else if you have an oak from an acorn you planted ages ago. The raging storms, the early freezes, the year the leaves turned brighter red than usual — all that is part of the oak you have raised yourself, or the oak you have watched over many years.

So time does make a difference in any garden. At first you wonder if anything will ever get large enough to count in the general picture. Then you wonder if there is any way to keep it from growing further. For years the little cunninghamia, say, a favorite shrub, then all of a sudden it becomes a small tree, then after a while you start thinking of it as a gnarled and marvelous fixture of the garden and can hardly think back to the time before you had it.

The great trick, I am now sure, is to flow with the tide.